Heinrich Kaan's
"Psychopathia Sexualis" (1844)

A volume in the series

Cornell Studies in the History of Psychiatry

Edited by Sander L. Gilman and George J. Makari

A list of titles in the series is available at
www.cornellpress.cornell.edu

Heinrich Kaan's "Psychopathia Sexualis" (1844)

A Classic Text in the History of Sexuality

Edited by Benjamin Kahan

Translated by Melissa Haynes

Cornell University Press

Ithaca and London

First published 2016 by Cornell University Press
First printing, Cornell Paperbacks, 2016

Printed in the United States of America

Library of Congress Cataloging-in-Publication Data

Names: Kaan, Heinrich, 1816-1893, author. | Kahan, Benjamin, editor. |
    Haynes, Melissa, translator.
Title: Heinrich Kaan's "Psychopathia sexualis" (1844) : a classic text in the
    history of sexuality / edited by Benjamin Kahan ; translated by Melissa
    Haynes.
Other titles: Psychopathia sexualis. English (Kahan) | Cornell studies in the
    history of psychiatry.
Description: Ithaca ; London : Cornell University Press, 2016. | Series:
    Cornell studies in the history of psychiatry | Includes bibliographical
    references and index.
Identifiers: LCCN 2016016900
ISBN 9781501704604 (cloth : alk. paper)
ISBN 9781501704611 (pbk. : alk. paper)
Subjects: LCSH: Sex (Psychology).
Classification: LCC HQ21 .K23 2016 | DDC 155.3—dc23
LC record available at https://lccn.loc.gov/2016016900

Cornell University Press strives to use environmentally responsible
suppliers and materials to the fullest extent possible in the publishing
of its books. Such materials include vegetable-based, low-VOC inks
and acid-free papers that are recycled, totally chlorine-free, or partly
composed of nonwood fibers. For further information, visit our website
at www.cornellpress.cornell.edu.

Cloth printing   10 9 8 7 6 5 4 3 2 1
Paperback printing   10 9 8 7 6 5 4 3 2 1

Contents

Editor's Acknowledgments   *vii*

Editor's Introduction: The First Sexology?   *1*

Translator's Note   *24*

Kaan's *Psychopathia Sexualis* **(1844)**   *27*

    Part 1   *37*

    Part 2   *84*

Appendix (Translation from German by
  Maya Vinokour)   *163*

Notes   *179*

Index   *191*

Editor's Acknowledgments

This book would never have begun were it not for Ian Cornelius's limitless intellectual curiosity and scholarly range. The project will always owe its first and greatest debt to him and his continued engagement. It also owes a great deal to the support of many institutions and individuals. I received support from Washington University in St. Louis, the Bill and Carol Fox Center for Humanistic Inquiry at Emory University, and the Humanities Center at the University of Pittsburgh. I am particularly grateful to Jonathan Arac, Randall Halle, and my fantastic research assistant, Ljudmila Bilkić, at Pitt. I finished this project with the help of the United States Studies Centre at the University of Sydney and several Wood Institute travel grants from the College of Physicians of Philadelphia. I am thankful for the continued support of Louisiana State University, which has so graciously let me pursue this project across many years and many cities. These travels have fostered and bestowed the precious gift of intellectual friendship. I cannot imagine a better set of readers than Chris Barrett, Michael Bibler, Ross Brooks, Andy Gaedtke, Greta LaFleur, Crystal Lake, Jeff Masten, Elsie Michie, and James Mulholland. They have all helped my introduction and edition enormously. Ivan Crozier's encyclopedic knowledge of sexology has enriched and deepened this project. Madoka Kishi's incomparable ability to see the field of sexuality studies in its entirety has helped me conceptualize and envision the project's largest theoretical stakes. On hearing of this undertaking, Liliane Weissberg immediately suggested Cornell University Press as the perfect venue for its publication, and I continue to be grateful for her wisdom in this matter. The team at Cornell has been wonderful to work with and my editor Kitty Hue-Tsung Liu's thoughtfulness has been a pleasure. I am grateful to my anonymous readers and my no-longer-anonymous readers, Pete Coviello and Beth Freeman, for their phenomenal suggestions. They have improved the book tremendously.

Heinrich Kaan's
"Psychopathia Sexualis" (1844)

The First Sexology?

HEINRICH KAAN'S
PSYCHOPATHIA SEXUALIS (1844)

> With Heinrich Kaan's book [*Psychopathia Sexualis*]
> we have then what could be called the date of birth, or
> in any case the date of the emergence, of sexuality and
> sexual aberrations in the psychiatric field.
>
> —Michel Foucault, *Abnormal: Lectures at
> the Collège de France, 1974–1975*

Heinrich Kaan is perhaps the most famous unknown figure in the history of sexuality. He is the author of what Michel Foucault calls "the first treatise of psychiatry to speak only of sexual psychopathology."[1] This critical edition of Kaan's *Psychopathia Sexualis* (1844) brings into English for the first time the text that more than any earlier text invented the modern regimes of sexuality. The significance of Kaan's virtually undiscovered yet essential text for the history of sexuality and the history of psychiatry is difficult to overstate since the text constitutes, in Foucault's phrase, "the first great global dynasty of sexual aberrations."[2] Foucault means that Kaan's *Psychopathia Sexualis* taxonomizes the normal and the abnormal, ordering sexuality in this abiding way for the first time. By providing sexuality with a new structure—imagination—that links all sexual acts together and that connects bodily instincts to the mind, Kaan suggests that sexuality produces a class of person. And by linking the sexual instinct to the imagination, Kaan forges what Foucault calls "a unified field of sexual abnormality."[3]

Kaan's taxonomy consists of six sexual aberrations: masturbation, pederasty, lesbian love, necrophilia, bestiality, and the violation of statues. This psychiatric field of relations between abnormalities of the mind and abnormalities of the body furnishes both the theoretical underpinnings for and the name of Richard von Krafft-Ebing's widely read and better-known *Psychopathia Sexualis* (1886). Although Kaan did not have many readers (because, among other reasons, he wrote in Latin), his impact on sexology, and on Iwan Bloch, Havelock Ellis, Auguste Ambroise Tardieu, Benjamin Tarnowsky, and particularly on Krafft-Ebing, is of immense importance. Kaan not only creates the field of sexology but plays a critical role in the regimes of knowledge production and discipline about psychiatric and sexual subjects. Of course, Kaan did not conjure sexology out of thin air. As I will argue, the medical literatures on syphilis and anti-onanism and the discourse of popular botany provided important precedents. Without Kaan's outline of a sexual nosography and innovations in case history, however, Krafft-Ebing would have been unable to establish his extensive system of sexual taxonomy.[4]

Kaan's work is much more than a historical precursor. As my epigraph begins to suggest, I hope that this new edition of Kaan's text will inaugurate a wholesale reconsideration of the historical emergence of the hetero/homo binary and sexual identity. In a lecture about Kaan, delivered in 1975 and translated into English in 2004, Foucault offers an alternative thesis to his extraordinarily well-known argument in *History of Sexuality* (1976) that the homosexual became a species in 1870, contending that sexuality emerged in 1844 with the publication of Kaan's text. Thus, this edition will allow a reassessment of the most famous claim in sexuality studies.

Since the publication of Foucault's *History of Sexuality*, it has become something of a critical commonplace in sexuality studies to note sexology's constitutive role in the formation of the hetero/homo divide. Devising such neologisms as "homosexuality," "heterosexuality," "sadism," and "masochism," sexology creates our vocabularies of sexuality and has had a determinative impact on our understanding of sexuality. Despite this commanding importance, Joseph Bristow has asserted that "it remains the case that even the more distinguished of the many historical accounts of sexual science repeatedly fail to tell us why this body of knowledge developed as it did."[5] While the more recent work of scholars like Heike Bauer, Lucy Bland and Laura Doan, Margot Canaday, Ivan Crozier, Kate Fisher, Jana Funke, Jay Prosser, Dana Seitler, Siobhan Somerville, and Jennifer Terry has begun to provide a course correction, Kaan's work is entirely left out of these accounts.[6] This edition rectifies Kaan's absence from the critical literature on sexology and has the potential to revamp our understanding of what Bristow calls the "urgent questions" of sexology's emergence.[7]

Kaan's multigenre treatise—part medical discourse, part sexual taxonomy, part psychiatric handbook, part activist statement, and part anti-onanist tract—provides a key piece of the puzzle in filling out sexology's formation. Moreover, what we understand as the multigenre quality of the text points to the inchoate nature of both psychiatry and sexology, drawing together several fields to create these two new disciplines. The text is written in Latin in part to lend these new fields intellectual seriousness and in part because the material was understood to be scandalous and rendering it in Latin kept it from wide readership. (This is a point made in Blumröder's review, reproduced in the appendix.)

This tradition of rendering objectionable material in Latin appears in contemporaneous anti-onanist literature, including John Todd's famous *Student's Manual* (1835).[8] In 1892, when an English-language translation of Krafft-Ebing's *Psychopathia Sexualis* appeared, some sections were presented in Latin; the *British Medical Journal* suggested the entire text should have been "veiled in the decent obscurity of a dead language."[9] An anonymous review of Kaan's text (reproduced here in the appendix) similarly describes Kaan's remarks on the perversions of the sexual instinct as "unsuitable for translation" (164) before quoting them in Latin.

Even as Latin shrouded sexual meaning, it also facilitated sexual articulation (as Foucault's repressive hypothesis teaches us) well into the twentieth century. Building on the work of David M. Halperin, Yopie Prins, and Linda Dowling, I understand classical learning as itself providing a vehicle for sexual expression and of sexual knowledge.[10] When Ralph Werther in *Autobiography of an Androgyne* (1918) wanted to describe sex acts, he used Latin. In 1930, when the English poet and classical scholar A. E. Housman sought to clarify "the meaning of various sexual acts mentioned in Roman literature . . . he chose to express himself in Latin rather than in English," and even so censors delayed publication of his work.[11] But the fact that Housman's essay eventually was published in Germany suggests that Latin provided a mode of expression at the border of the unspeakable. Inquiring about the sex lives of two women in 1822, Anne Lister asked "if they were classical."[12] This understanding of the classical as a mode of knowledge is also evident when Herculine Barbin used Ovid's *Metamorphoses* as a way to understand her hermaphroditism at the end of the nineteenth century.[13] Classical learning then, provided a parallel knowledge and language of sexuality that ran alongside sexology, but it also informed sexology, providing its Latinate diction, classical imagery, and even—as Kaan's text suggests—its language of articulation.

In the remainder of this introduction, I will detail what is known of Kaan's life and chart three central discursive and institutional contexts by which his text is shaped and with which it engages: the intellectual atmosphere of the University of Vienna and its theories of psychiatry, the anti-onanism movement, and the adaptations of Linnaean plant taxonomy. These three tributary discourses—Viennese psychiatry, anti-onanism, and Linnaean taxonomy—each contribute to the development of the early history of sexology and of Kaan's text in particular.

The Life of Heinrich Kaan

Kaan was born in Vienna on February 8, 1816, the son of a successful wholesale merchant. His ethnic identity is disputed, in part because he describes himself on the title page of *Psychopathia Sexualis* as "*medicus ruthenicus*." Volkmar Sigusch understands him to be Austrian, arguing that "*medicus ruthenicus*" should be translated "Russian physician," and sees the epithet "Russian" as no more than a description of Kaan's work at the St. Petersburg women's hospital (Frauen-Hospital) where he wrote *Psychopathia Sexualis*.[14] That is, Sigusch contends that Kaan did not intend to claim any Russian or Ruthenian ethnic heritage. In 1825, however, Kaan did change identities, converting from Judaism to Catholicism. Kaan's father had converted a few months earlier, in late 1824. At the beginning of 1825, Kaan's three youngest sisters followed their father in conversion. Then Kaan and the rest of his siblings, with the exception of his eldest brother, converted as well.[15] This conversion was very likely a matter of practicality. Assimilation and marriage interdictions between couples of mixed background made conversion especially attractive in Vienna. As Marsha Rozenblit argues, "Vienna's Jewish conversion rate far outranked that of any other city in the Dual Monarchy or elsewhere in Europe."[16] About half of Jewish Viennese converts became Catholics like Kaan. Moreover, many male converts were professionals since conversion facilitated career advancement among the well-to-do.[17]

This conversion may have helped him gain acceptance to the prestigious Akademisches Gymnasium of Vienna (run by the Piarist Order). Kaan attended from 1826 to 1832 and then studied philosophy from 1832 to 1834. He studied medicine at the University of Vienna from 1834 to 1839. While many facts of Kaan's life are sketchy, he is known to have been in St. Petersburg from 1848 to 1849, during a cholera outbreak. He treated patients there and was inspired to write *A Physician's Thoughts about Cholera as World-Epidemic* (1854). In 1850, Kaan returned to Austria and immediately began a several-month observation at the Spital der Barmherzigen Schwestern in Leopoldstadt, under the direction of the self-described homeopath Franz Wurmb. Kaan had been interested in homeopathic medicine from the beginning of his medical studies. This interest in homeopathy is evident in *Psychopathia Sexualis*'s dedication to Martin Mandt as Mandt was an advocate for small doses of drugs. Despite Kaan having used homeopathic means to successfully treat himself for a heart condition when he was a student, he had lingering doubts about the homeopathic system. That changed in St. Petersburg when he saw how successfully homeopathy was used in the treatment of typhoid patients, which led him to end his treatise on cholera with a plea for homeopathy. *Psychopathia Sexualis* registers Kaan's oscillating feelings about homeopathy.[18]

After leaving St. Petersburg, Kaan lived and worked in Meran and Innsbruck from about 1851 to 1864. During this period, he worked at a military hospital in Innsbruck and wrote several books for tourists of the Alps. In the preface to "Ischl and Its Region" (1875), Kaan reviewed his life writing: "Fate drove me from the blue Danube to the banks of the Newa, where, for 10 years, I enjoyed the amiability and hospitality of the residents of that great northern metropolis, St. Petersburg. Family bonds detained me in Meran and Innsbruck, and much of my intellectual work owes its existence to these circumstances. Old Juvavia became my new homeland, and my new earthly paradise grew up along the banks of the Salzach River, in New Salzburg [Neusalzburg]."[19] Beginning in either 1862 or 1864, Kaan arrived in Ischl and took a very active role in the administration of the Ischl health resort, practicing medicine there until the end of his life. Kaan died in Vienna on May 24, 1893, and was survived by his wife, a son, and a daughter. His son, Hans Kaan, was also a physician and may have been cited by Freud as "Dr. Hanns Kaan" in "A Case of Successful Treatment by Hypnotism" (1892–1893), though the identification cannot be established with certainty. Kaan's daughter, Helene Kaan, wrote a brief memoir about the famed Austrian writer Karl Kraus. The two met in 1904, became romantically involved, and remained friends until Kraus's death.[20]

The Viennese Context

In the nineteenth century, Vienna was "the world epicenter of medicine."[21] While a great deal is known about fin-de-siècle Viennese psychiatry and the intellectual contexts of such luminaries as Krafft-Ebing and Freud, relatively little has been written about the late eighteenth- and early nineteenth-century traditions of psychiatry that would decisively impact Heinrich Kaan. For example, the eminent historian of science, Magda Whitrow, began her article

"The Early History of the Vienna Psychiatric Clinic" (1990) in the year 1870, more than twenty-five years after Kaan's most famous writing.[22] Indeed, as Whitrow rightly pointed out, psychiatry was a very young discipline in 1870. Johann Friedreich compiled the first substantial German-language bibliography of psychiatric literature in 1833.[23] As Eric J. Engstrom has argued, this was an important step in disciplinary consolidation and autonomy and enabled the first professional organizations and journals to emerge at midcentury.[24]

To the extent that psychiatry had a disciplinary history before 1870, Vienna was an important locale. Like Krafft-Ebing and Freud, Kaan was affiliated with the University of Vienna, which was arguably the most important European medical institution of the nineteenth century. As noted, Kaan studied medicine there from 1834 to 1839, possibly taking a year off to study in Padua from 1837 to 1838. In November 1840 he stood for his viva voce exam in obstetrics, and in December he was accepted into the medical faculty at the University of Vienna. This period witnessed the end of the reign of the dictatorial and reactionary Joseph Andreas von Stifft over the Vienna Medical School (1803–1836) and the flowering of a new era after his death in 1836.[25]

At the end of the eighteenth century, before Stifft, the Vienna Medical School was at the forefront of developments in psychiatry. The Narrenturm ("fool's tower"), constructed in 1784, was one of the earliest European psychiatric hospitals and was recognized "as an exemplary solution for its time."[26] During this period, Dr. Franz Joseph Gall (1758–1828) developed his new science of the skull—cranioscopy (later called "phrenology")—in Vienna. Gall hoped that fingering the elevations and depressions of the scalp would enable him to discern the attributes, defects, and character of its owner. However, by 1798 Gall observed, "The object of my investigations is the brain: the skull only inasmuch as it is a faithful reproduction of the surface of the brain and therefore only a part of the main object."[27] This shift from the skull to the brain opened what Erna Lesky calls "the door to a new field of endeavor," making the study of the mind into a "subject of exact analytical research methods."[28] Additionally, this new development underwrote the possibility of seeing the brain as a pathological seat for mental illness at precisely the moment when the study of pathological anatomy was gaining increasing stature in Vienna.

These developments were extremely important for Kaan as the intellectual contexts out of which his psychiatric work would emerge. Pathological anatomy with its emphasis on abnormality became a further influence; he describes the field in *Psychopathia Sexualis*, asserting that it "sheds so much light over the vast field of disease" (154). In 1796, the Vienna Medical School founded a museum of pathological anatomy and created an unsalaried prosector's post for the professional display of cadavers. In 1811, this post became salaried, and in 1821 it was raised to an associate professorship. From 1818, the prosector performed all the hospital's postmortems and (quite unusually) all the city's forensic autopsies.[29] These significant institutional changes established Vienna as a world leader in pathological anatomy, as no other chair in this field (with the exception of one at the University of Strasbourg) yet existed. One reason pathological anatomy rose to such prominence in Vienna was the ready supply of corpses. In contrast to the United States, England, France, and Germany, where strenuous objections to dissection limited medical schools' access to corpses, Vienna had a ready supply. The young Irish physician William Wilde, Oscar Wilde's father, remarked of Vienna in 1840: "There are many opportunities to gain knowledge in this area [anatomy] as the supply with dissectible bodies is plentiful."[30] Indeed, many

British and US medical students came to Vienna to access the Viennese supply of cadavers. As Tatjana Buklijas argues, Vienna was in the unusual position of having a "medical and death culture strongly shaped by Roman Catholicism, cultural connections with Italian centres, and [a] vision of society advanced by absolutist monarchs."[31] Buklijas contends that because many Viennese practitioners from the mid-sixteenth century on were trained in Italy (as Kaan probably was), Vienna shared Italy's Catholic culture of death in which "death was a quick and radical separation of the soul from the body."[32] Moreover, Austria's emperor Joseph II took the utilitarian view that "the use of patients' bodies in medical education [was] a fair repayment for the free medical care they had received in the hospital."[33]

The ready supply of corpses enabled Karl Rokitansky (whom Kaan holds up as an exemplary doctor in his text) to dissect between 25,000 and 30,000 corpses over the course of his career.[34] Joining the faculty in 1833, Rokitansky became a leading light in Vienna, and by 1844 (the year of Kaan's text) he was a full professor of pathological anatomy.[35] It would be difficult to overestimate Rokitansky's influence on the development of the field of pathological anatomy; one of his successors would refer to him as "the Linnaeus of pathological anatomy."[36]

In his foundational essay "Closing Up the Corpses," Arnold I. Davidson argues that central to "psychiatry's emergence, in the nineteenth century, as an autonomous medical discipline" was the decline of pathological anatomy: "Pathological anatomy could not serve psychiatry either as an explanatory theory for so-called mental diseases or disorders or as the foundation for the classification and description of these diseases."[37] Kaan exemplifies Davidson's thesis: he moves away from pathological anatomy, deciding, as he says in *Psychopathia Sexualis*, that "genital organs marked with a pathological anatomy are not worthy of that attention that is accorded the other organs" (154).

Davidson divides the history of sexual perversion into three overlapping stages, each of which is characterized by its own mode or form of explanation. The first stage located perversion as a disease of the reproductive or sexual organs. The second stage saw the neurophysiology and neuroanatomy of the brain as the seat of perversion. These two stages of explanation shared an epistemology rooted in pathological anatomy. The third stage, however, decisively broke from the first two, by taking root in psychology rather than anatomy. In order to underwrite such a shift (from organ to instinct), Davidson argues that there must be and in fact was "virtually *unargued unanimity*" about the proper function of the sexual instinct—propagation—so that functional disturbances could be delineated.[38] One reason Foucault finds Kaan's text so important is that (though he does not use these terms) it is the first text to exhibit this third stage of psychological etiology, and thus laid the foundation for the emergence of the psychiatric model of modern sexuality. I will say more about this foundation later, but for now it is important to note that Kaan's text exhibits all three of Davidson's overlapping explanatory stages:

> The brain and genital system hold themselves in the following way: as two poles that are engaged in constant action and reciprocal reaction. Thus, in *Psychopathia sexualis*, the imagination breaks the will of a man, even if his rational mind rejects and reviles this deed. (94)

In addition to these three centers that are all in some sense interior to the body, Kaan also attributes sexuality in part to environmental and other external factors.

This environmental thinking about sexuality came to Vienna via Johann Peter Frank's encounter with the Scottish physician John

Brown. Brown's theories of excitability (known as Brunonian-ism) understood disease to result from either excessive or deficient amounts of stimulation. By 1804, Brunonianism had collapsed and was replaced by a moderate version of natural philosophy under Philipp Carl Hartmann's chairmanship of general pathology, therapy, and materia medica in 1811. Hartmann has been called "the source" "of Vienna psychology and psychiatry."[39] We can see his insistence that environmental forces be grounded in organic processes at work in Kaan's system of sexuality. In Kaan's discussion of the onset of puberty (which is linked for him to the emergence of sexuality), for example, he sees puberty developing "sooner in hot regions," "later in inhabitants of the countryside," and more rapidly when food is "plentiful, heat producing, and moist" (63). Such climatic thinking about sexuality had a long afterlife—evident, most famously, in Richard Burton's theorization of the Sotadic Zone in 1886. Even as late as 1940, Eugen Steinach could describe the "sex life" of inhabitants of "warm latitudes" as manifesting "more intensive and rapid development than in the more temperate zones."[40]

Environmental thought was only one important influence on Kaan. The period during which he studied at the University of Vienna witnessed extraordinary intellectual changes. After the 1836 death of the powerful and conservative Stifft, his son-in-law Johann Nepomuk Raimann succeeded him. Raimann lacked energy in his new role of protomedicus, creating an opening for reform. Ludwig Baron von Türkheim seized this opportunity, creating the Vienna Society of Physicians and beginning the revolutionary reorganization of the Vienna Medical School that would occur in 1848. The Vienna Society of Physicians provided a forum for a "wealth of opinions" and lively debate. While it is not known whether Kaan was a member during his tenure, this organization undoubtedly influenced the atmosphere of his studies.[41]

The conservatism of Stifft's leadership meant that by 1844, the German psychiatrist Heinrich Damerow could write of Vienna: "The Imperial City still lacks an institution for the treatment and care of the mentally ill—an institution that would befit its dignity and compare with the magnificence of other institutions. . . . Vienna at present possesses not a single outstanding personality in the field of psychiatry."[42] In 1839, the Narrenturm removed its chains, but kept its other appliances for mechanical restraint (straitjackets, belts, restraining chairs, etc.), making it vulnerable to charges like Damerow's that it embodied anachronistic thinking. This rearguard environment emphasizes the singularity of Kaan's achievement.[43]

Anti-Onanism

In spite of this uniqueness, the text's preoccupation with the ills of masturbation makes it simultaneously very much a text of its time. Kaan makes no ordinary attack on the evils of masturbation, but rather effects a fundamental shift in the understanding of masturbation and its entwinement with the history of the subject. Thomas Laqueur's monumental *Solitary Sex* (2003) argues that "masturbation is the sexuality of the [modern] self par excellence."[44] Laqueur understands masturbation to encapsulate simultaneously all the hopes of the Enlightenment and its greatest fears. For example, while modernity values individuality and self-determination, masturbation threatens self-absorption and loss of meaningful contact with other people.[45] Even as Laqueur makes bold claims for masturbation's crucial positioning at the intersection of Enlightenment thought and its gothic underbelly, Kaan's text amazingly demonstrates that Laqueur actually underestimates the importance of masturbation to the modern self.

By linking masturbation to the other aberrations in his taxonomy, Kaan's text forges an intellectual genealogy from anti-onanist literature to the birth of sexology and its accompanying rubrics and languages of sex and sexuality.

In claiming that sexology emerges directly from anti-onanism, I draw on the important work of Eve Sedgwick, who hypothesizes that masturbation was "uniquely formative" in the construction of sexual identities: "the masturbator may have been at the cynosural center of a remapping of individual identity."[46] Kaan's *Psychopathia Sexualis* fills in the details of Sedgwick's supposition that the masturbator was one of many sexual identities "subsumed, erased, or overrriden" by the hetero/homo binary.[47] We can see how a preoccupation with the regulation of homosexuality in the later nineteenth and early twentieth century replaced an obsession with masturbation in the eighteenth and early nineteenth century.

Kaan's *Psychopathia Sexualis* pioneers four propositions that lay the foundation for this tectonic shift from the regulation of sexuality through masturbation to regulation focused on homosexuality. The first technique—which Foucault calls "decompartmentalization"[48]—fuses masturbation, homosexuality, and Kaan's other perversions together:

> In every distortion of the sexual instinct, it is the imagination that supplies the path that fulfills it, contrary to the laws of nature. All these types of deviation are merely different forms of one and the same thing, and they cross into one another. Boys who are given to onanism, even if dissuaded from this habit at a later age, most easily fall into other aberrations of the sexual drive; and among primitive peoples, one type occurs at the same time with others (82).

Kaan's text sets the stage for masturbation and homosexuality to bleed into one another ("all these types of deviation are merely different forms of one and the same thing"), enabling the demise of antimasturbation rhetoric as a mode of discipline and the rise of the regulation of homosexuality as its replacement in maintaining the social order. While Kaan is far more concerned with masturbation than any of the other aberrations in his taxonomy, his text accents masturbation differently than his predecessors, imagining it as alloerotic (or threatening to be so) as well as autoerotic. Onanism, for Kaan, ceases to be merely a problem in and of itself (of dissipation, of self-control, of self-absorption—though it also poses these dangers) and instead obtains a new and crucial position as a kind of gateway to other vices, occurring, Kaan says, "at the same time with others [aberrations]" and "cross[ing] into one another." This newly hierarchized understanding of masturbation suggests that guarding against onanism is tantamount to the prevention of other aberrations of the sexual instinct. Once Kaan's text opens the possibility that masturbation and other aberrations (especially homosexuality) are terms in a sequence, the movement from Kaan's position that onanism facilitates or occurs at the same time with other aberrations to a position in which those other aberrations are themselves the central problem requires only a shift in emphasis and enables us to see how the hetero/homo binary replaced the cynosural center of masturbation. In short, Kaan's text enables us to see how sexuality becomes primarily alloerotic.

The relation between fantasy and practice in this shift is a key part of this story and one that brings us to Kaan's second proposition which conceives the sexual instinct as always overflowing its natural aim toward procreation in the form of what he calls "imagination." As Foucault points out, "It is natural for the instinct to be abnormal" in Kaan's conception.[49] While Kaan's text offers very little that could be perceived as antihomophobic or queer, this constitutive abnormality serves as a resource for queer theory, one that might read Kaan's text against the grain to find the universality of queerness in the sexual instinct.[50] Latter-day sexologists like Albert Schrenck-Notzing take up this proposition, arguing that "every single onanistic act must overcome reality, and thus a much more intense strain of the imagination is necessary. . . . [Masturbation] brings onanists into a peculiar and, I might say, unphysiological relation to the opposite sex. In that it destroys the sexual relation with the opposite sex, it weakens sexual desire and attacks the most powerful natural instinct—love's impulse—at its very root."[51] Here, masturbation's power to overcome reality unthreads the "normal" relations between the sexes and the "natural instinct" of love. To put this differently, masturbation destroys heterosexuality and breeds queerness, helping us to see how Kaan's linking of the imagination and the sexual instinct enables the shift from masturbation to homosexuality at the cynosural center of sexual identity. This "privileged link" between imagination and instinct is important to Foucault and to the history of psychiatry for another reason:

> Whereas instinct was at this time essentially invoked as the support of habitual, irresistible, and automatic actions unaccompanied by thoughts, the sexual instinct actually described by Heinrich Kaan is strictly linked to imagination. It is imagination that opens up the space in which instinct will be able to develop its abnormal nature. The effects of the uncoupling of nature and normality are revealed in the imagination, and it is on this basis that the imagination serves as the intermediary or relay of the causal and pathological effectiveness of the sexual instinct.[52]

In this relay, Foucault suggests that Kaan moves sexuality away from the realm of merely somatic disorders and instead is able to posit the mind as the seat of sexuality. This psychiatric concept of imagination thus locates perversion as a natural part of subjectivity and one that arises in all subjects. Moreover, this universality

of perversion makes it a powerful conduit of regulation and expands psychiatry's ability to perform such a disciplinary function
(in both senses). The most important innovation of this fusion of
imagination and instinct, however, is the way it lays the foundation for finding a sexual basis for phenomena that are not on their
face sexual; Kaan explains in *Psychopathia Sexualis* that the sexual
instinct "commands all of life" (69). This suggestion propounds a
tremendous widening of the sexual sphere, one that places sexual
life at the center of human experience.

Kaan recasts the life stage of sexual experience, emphasizing
childhood as a privileged developmental stage for sexual etiology
and constituting our third proposition.—namely, Kaan's explo-
ration of what Foucault calls childhood's "determining value in
the etiology of illness."[53] This emphasis on childhood marks a key
difference with his sexological descendants—Krafft-Ebing, Bloch,
and Ellis—who privilege puberty, and places him much closer
to Freud and his emphasis on infantile sexuality.[54] For Kaan, the
clearest proof of sexuality's exceeding its function of copulation
is found in childhood games that are gender differentiated and in
children's curiosity about their own sexual organs and those of
other children of both sexes. These manifestations of play and
curiosity suggest that the sexual instinct is, as Foucault explains,
"much too lively, precocious, and wide, and it too easily passes
through the whole organism and conduct of individuals to be able
to really lodge and take place solely in adult heterosexual copulation."[55] Childhood is a privileged age and onanism is a privileged
sexual aberration because "premature desires" incited by masturbation prepare the way, as Foucault says, "for all the sexual aberrations," helping the imagination look for "additional, derivative, or
substitute means of satisfaction."[56] To put this more plainly, childhood masturbation is the wellspring for all sexual aberration.

Finally, Kaan's innovations within the genre of the sexual case history enable imagination to generate varieties of personhood. The medical literature on syphilis—with its emphasis on heredity, disease, sexual drives, and the visibility of sexuality—provides an important ancestor to Kaan's sexual case history. He understands sexual psychopathology to encourage and render "the attack of the venereal disease [syphilis] of longer duration or more perilous" (137). In addition to warning against the dangers of syphilis, he draws on the syphilitic medical literature's conjuration of the visibility of sexuality—the way that syphilis is imagined to be written on the body. Since at least as far back as the sixteenth century, as Sander L. Gilman argues, "the face [of the syphilitic] becomes the sign of the genitalia."[57] In addition, syphilis is located in the mind by the end of the seventeenth century. Gervais Uçay was the first to recognize that syphilis caused not only physical ills but also "those of the mind, which also appear to be extremely bizarre in countless different ways."[58] Thus, syphilis was a sexual disease that was located both in the body and the mind. Kaan builds on this work in his case studies of sexual personhood, forging sexual subjects who are discernible by outward signs and symptoms, but who crucially have diseased imaginations.

These four technical innovations—around the process of decompartmentalization, the sex instinct, childhood, and the case study—work together to implant perversion in the subject, making possible what Foucault has theorized as the speciation of homosexuality. A genealogy of this speciation is particularly important for sexuality studies, but it also has broad implications for questions of nation, race, gender, and citizenship. These issues are very much in the foreground of Kaan's case studies, particularly the long case study with which the text closes:

> Mauritius S. . . . , a young man of eighteen years, of Jewish origin, who later embraced the Christian faith, already as a child excelled with a

premature sharpness of the mind. On account of the generosity and kindness of his soul, throughout the entire short course of his life, he was loved greatly by his parents and by everyone who knew him. At first, he was dedicated to his letters and studies, then sought a military career, and with highest success executed his military service in such a way that the testimony of his professors designated him among the outstanding young men at that place. . . . I do not know whether it was in the gymnasium or later in the military institution that he became given over to onanism, but it can be assumed, since already as a boy he presented clear symptoms of *Psychopathia sexualis*. His premature puberty and way of life certainly contributed much to developing the diseased seed. The attack of the disease sufficiently indicated its origin from this source, like a serpent afflicting all his organs and systems, making every therapy vain, even harmful. (155–56)

While Robert Beachy credits Johann Ludwig Caspar as the author of "the first scientific case study of a sodomite" (a characterization with which I agree), Mauritius S's association with the homoerotic spaces of the gymnasium and the military as well as the association of onanism with homosexuality mark, I would contend, Mauritius S's case as an important precursor.[59] After Mauritius S's death, Kaan understands the cause of his sexual psychopathology to stem from the patient's "eastern origin." Kaan's racialization of disease here reinforces the claims made by Sander L. Gilman, Siobhan Somerville, and Estelle Freedman, who have mapped the racial underpinnings of sexology, psychoanalysis, and the biological sciences more generally.[60] It is the discourse of botany, however, that naturalizes these new categories of sexual personhood for Kaan.

The Botany of Desire

Kaan's understanding of sexuality is rooted in botany. I borrow Michael Pollan's phrase (though not his sense) "the botany of desire" to describe Kaan's meditation on botany as a language of sex.[61] Botany was taught as part of the first-year curriculum at the Vienna Medical School, and it provides a critical vocabulary for Kaan's sexual taxonomy.[62] Kaan reconfigures Linnaeus's plant taxonomy (which Linnaeus based on the number and arrangement of plants' sexual organs) to theorize human sexuality. I contend that botany not only provided a language of sex before the invention of sexology, as Greta L. LaFleur brilliantly argues, but also that Kaan played a crucial role in transforming the language of botany into a formal discourse of sexology.[63] He revalues the Linnaean emphasis on reproductive systems as a convenient and largely inconsequential principle of ordering to produce a system of sexual taxonomy and pathology. Kaan primarily seizes on and recasts Linnaeus's idea of "function":

> The organic body reproduces itself not only internally but also externally. Internal reproduction is seen in the act of nutrition and involves a *series of functions* that are simpler in less advanced organic bodies than in those that are more advanced and closer to human nature. External reproduction is seen in the act of generation, which obeys the same laws as nutrition; in lower beings, it is simpler and in higher beings, more advanced. (my emphasis, 38)

As Davidson has helped us see, this emphasis on function departs from an anatomical basis and underwrites the psychiatric origins of sexuality.[64] Kaan's text does not quite put forward a "psychic manifestation" of sexuality, but rather marks an important conjunction between, on the one hand, a perception of human sexuality on a continuum with other natural processes (especially those of plants) and, on the other, a sexual instinct that "overflows its natural end and does so naturally."[65] Instead, this "series of functions" produces what Foucault calls "the dynamic manifestation of the functioning of the sexual organs."[66] This dynamic manifestation consists of "a feeling" or "impression"—something akin to hunger.[67] Kaan's theorization of the sexual instinct as a kind of drive like hunger entails, as Foucault says, "a very marked naturalization of human sexuality."[68]

Botany was so thoroughly sexualized during this period that it bordered on the pornographic; this was noticed by contemporaries, such as the *Encyclopaedia Britannica*, which sniffed haughtily: "[a] man would not naturally expect to meet with disgusting strokes of obscenity in a system of botany . . . [but] . . . obscenity is the very basis of the Linnaean system."[69] Christa Knellwolf draws out these connections, arguing that the word "exotic," which we associate today with both foreignness and sensuality, in the eighteenth century referred mainly to plants. In other words, it functioned more as a noun than as an adjective, describing a category of things, rather than a quality. With this proximity between botany and sex in mind, we might position Kaan in a genealogy that runs all the way from Erasmus Darwin's (and Anna Seward's) *The Loves of the Plants* (1789) to 1920s and 30s gay slang that nominates effeminate men "horticultural lads" and names them after flowers: "pansy," "daisy," and "buttercup."[70] The interarticulation of plants and sexuality is also evident in literary works by Charles Baudelaire, Walt Whitman, Emily Dickinson, Marc-André Raffalovich, Sarah Orne Jewett, and Marcel Proust, as well as Iwan Bloch's *Odoratus Sexualis*, Richard Burton's *Perfumed Garden*, and much of the work of Georgia O'Keeffe.[71] Roughly contemporaneous with Kaan's text, Whitman's "I Saw in Louisiana a Live-Oak Growing" features a speaker whose observations of the live oak become observations of himself: "I saw in Louisiana a live-oak growing. . . . Without any companion it grew there uttering joyous leaves of dark green, / And its look, rude, unbending, lusty, made me think of myself." The lustiness of the tree and the way in which later in this formally queer sonnet (containing thirteen lines) the tree will inspire thoughts of "manly love," suggests that for Whitman Linnaean taxonomy was a mode of self-understanding, a way of classifying, explaining, and expressing his homosexuality. Similarly, the amateur sexologist Ralph Werther writes in his *Autobiography of an Androgyne* (1918): "Contrary to the ordinary view, there exists, in the human race, no sharp dividing line between the sexes, just as there exists none between the vegetable and the animal kingdoms."[72] While Werther's analogy here seems to be a mere vehicle, Kaan's text demonstrates the extent to which the early history and emergence of sexuality is deeply structured by its engagement with botany. This botanical system of sexual ordering opens new commerce between sexuality studies, ecocriticism, and animal studies, enabling us to ask both how an originary relation to vegetation might reorient our bedrock assumptions about sexuality and how indebted our notions of human sexuality are to the study of the natural world around us. If sexuality is *the* secret of the self, then at the core of the human subject, according to Kaan, we find flora, suggesting the extent to which we are constituted in relation to and in perpetual dialogue with other species and even other biological kingdoms.[73]

This genealogy suggests that although Kaan inaugurates our understandings of sexuality and his categories are recognizable in our own, they are certainly not reducible to them. For example, Kaan defines lesbianism as "an aberration that consists in the satisfaction of the sexual drive either between men or between women by means of tribadism, or rubbing" (79). Such a description is particularly striking in light of Baudelaire's reference to "the male Sappho" in "Lesbos" (1845) and Aldous Huxley's *Antic Hay* (1923), in which he uses the term "lesbian" to describe licentious male-female sexual relations.[74] Kaan's text might help us begin to trace how the lesbian became a woman and opens the possibility of new and surprising intersections between gay and lesbian sex.[75] But the description of male same-sex acts under the sign of lesbianism might suggest the perceived effeminacy of male-male contact or a connection to the older history of the word "lesbianism" meaning "sensuality."[76] Likewise, Kaan's mention of "the satisfaction of lust with statues" (78), a formulation that the text never revisits, became a mainstay of sexological thought. Ellis coins the term "Pygmalionism" for "falling in love with statues," Krafft-Ebing includes violation of statues in his *Psychopathia Sexualis*, and Bloch states: "The peculiar relation which persons can form with statues is well known."[77] The luminous strangeness of moments like these in Kaan's wide-ranging text make it fascinating at nearly every moment, creating new intersections in the history of sexuality and psychiatry. It is my hope that this text will estrange our familiar understandings of sexuality and help us see just how unfamiliar sexuality and its science are to us.

Translator's Note

In my English translation, Heinrich Kaan's original footnotes have been retained as footnotes. In those cases where Kaan used a language other than Latin, I kept the original term, set it in italics, and, if more than a single word, translated the phrase or passage. Endnotes provide comments or clarifications made by the editor or me, and are set apart from the main work in order to allow the original structure of Kaan's text to remain clear. Throughout, *Psychopathia sexualis* has been kept as a quasi-medical diagnostic term as Kaan seems to have intended it to be used and understood.

Kaan deploys certain key terms in his description of the symptomatic suite that he sees in *Psychopathia sexualis,* including "sexual instinct" (*nisus sexualis*), "mental" or "psychical" versus "physical temperament" (*psychicum temperamentum, physicum temperamentum*), and "plastic" or "organic life" (*vita plastica*). This last term overlaps with the more common early medical and scientific idea of *vis plastica*, the formative force in nature that causes organic life to generate out of inorganic matter. Kaan sees a type of energy in higher-order animals that he terms *vita plastica*, that is, organic life. The first instance of these terms is marked in the translation with the original Latin in brackets (e.g., [*nisus sexualis*]).

I think that it is fair to say that I have read Kaan's Latin text more often and more closely than he could have anticipated. We have been odd bedfellows for almost seven years, and the project has followed wherever my peripatetic career has taken me. The time and attention that could be spared for this work was supported and furthered by a number of postdoctoral fellowships. I started my work on translating Kaan at Washington University in St. Louis as a Mellon Postdoctoral Fellow in Modeling Interdisciplinary Inquiry (2008–2010), did major revisions on the text at the University of Wisconsin-Madison as an ACLS New Faculty Fellow (2011–2013), and substantially finished my work while at Princeton University and Bucknell University as visiting faculty. In each place, it has been a pleasure to share this unusual and provocative text with colleagues, to ask them questions about neo-Latin and debate the use of Classics in nineteenth-century medical and scientific literature as a point of reception. I extend particular thanks to Kathryn Topper and Jarrett Welsh for all the support they have offered over these years, and to Jarrett for always having at the ready a nineteenth-century journal article on medical miscellany to help my reading of Kaan.

PSYCHOPATHIA

~

SEXUALIS

~

by the author HEINRICH KAAN

Russian Physician and Doctor of Medicine at Vienna

Etc. Etc.[1]

Leipzig

Leopold Voss

1844

Quem te Deus esse jussit et humana qua parte in locutus es in re, Disce.

Persius, *Sat.* III. v. 10[2]

The proper study of mankind is man.

Pope's *Essay on man*[3]

Que suis-je, où suis-je, et d'où suis-je tiré?

Voltaire[4]

To the most illustrious

Martin Mandt

Doctor of medicine and surgery, Senior Consulting

Physician to the Emperor of All Russia, etc. etc.

This book has been dedicated

with all due respect and esteem[5]

The Author

Preface

Neither a passion for writing nor an untimely and irresponsible fancy imposed on me the duty of entrusting such a difficult topic to a scholarly treatise (a subject of such importance and in which I am experienced)—and, moreover, to entrust it to public judgment. I have hardly escaped the snares that hindered my predecessors, nor do I know if my fate will be the same as theirs. But my intention was good. If this little treatise of mine does not meet every expectation, then I ask my reader to be satisfied with the present study and to expect more from future studies, since I have resolved, above all, to invest my life's work in research on this material.[6]

Roused by a certain instinct, I submitted to this danger. Since rather early in my studies this subject captured my attention. Even in the first years of my academic career numerous cases happened to present themselves before my eyes. After I took my degree, I became daily more convinced of the importance of this matter.[7] The great number of the sick whom everywhere I saw corrupted by this disease; the false but commonly held ideas about it; the small number of doctors who take an energetic interest in it; the as yet smaller number of books that have been written on this disease—all of these aroused in me a desire to collect case studies, to examine them and from them deduce general principles, and then to apply to them every kind of theoretical and practical knowledge and, thus, to derive from them rules useful to physicians. It was no doubt with feeble strength that I dared to pursue this end. At the beginning I set myself two objectives: first, to bring the severity of this disease to the attention of physicians; and second, to direct their attention to this subject in particular so that I might do my utmost to correct the errors and false ideas held by the public.

I have prepared this little treatise in Latin because I judge it too dangerous to hand over to the general public such a slippery matter before its utility and integrity can be proven. For this reason I prefer to write in the custom of scholars. If expert judgment does not totally reject my nights spent in toil, then I shall have the opportunity to publish my little treatise translated into a vernacular language such as French.[8]

I have collected primarily cases of *Psychopathia sexualis* in the masculine sex, for I freely admit that I have had little experience of this disease in the inferior sex.[9] Consequently, I leave that part for future investigations—for what good is it simply to copy others' books? I certainly do not want to be ranked among the plagiarists, of which our age already has far too many.[10]

Because there are already available numerous and good enough works on anamnestics and diagnostics, I have set forth a more general program of therapy. I have done so, moreover, because I intend this book more for my colleagues in the art of medicine than for the general public.[11] Under the light of critical reasoning, I attempted to survey the writings of the most eminent men such as Schoenlein and Neumann.[12] It is wrong to think that I dared to censure these men from whose works I have drawn so much for my own use. I have merely tried to draw out their opinions from their few words that touched on our subject and to put their opinions more clearly before the reader's eyes.

I have voluntarily disregarded Lallemand's therapy (as well as that of many others) given that I lack experience with the use of the instrument he invented and proposed.[13] My theoretical perspective, in any case, dissuades me from the application of this remedy. How could I—just a young doctor, still lacking the public trust and not holding a public office—venture such a heroic remedy (and one for which I find no sign that it should even be applied)? For reasons to be presented later, I have also omitted the subjects of symptomatic therapy and pathological anatomy.[14] I seek indulgence for my barely elegant Latin. I have neither been particularly intent on study of the Latin language, nor have I had sufficient time to devote the requisite attention to writing. At any rate, I have done what my abilities allowed, and in this regard I am not ashamed to plead for the reader's extreme indulgence and goodwill.

In all other respects, it is with an undaunted spirit that I hand my little treatise over to the just and honest judgment of scholars.

St. Petersburg, the 21st day of February, 1844
The AUTHOR

Index

Preface   (31)

Part 1   (37)

Explanation of the sexual system in plants (37); in animals (43); in the human species (43)

On Puberty (62). Physico-anatomical development in the young male (64). Physico-anatomical development in the female (65). Physico-physiological development in both sexes (66). Psychological development at the age of puberty (67)

On the sexual instinct (69)

What is *Psychopathia sexualis*? (81)

Part 2   (84)

The etiology of disease (84). Description of the Pathology (90). Diagnosis (95). Prognosis (98)

Therapy (100). Method for Psychological Cure (102); Method for Physical Cure (103); Method for Dietary Cure (104). Radical therapy (125).

Secondary diseases (135); according to age (136); temperament (139). On mental diseases (146). On sex (149).

Pathological anatomy (154)

Part 1

Explanation of the Sexual System in Plants

Every living being, which modern philosophers call an organic body, is generated by an agitation or motion of nature or, as natural scientists say, by some process. This living being is entirely contained by this motion and dies together with it. In fact, every inorganic thing is the final outcome (*Resultat*) of a process and persists after that action has been completed. In inorganic bodies such a process is more clearly visible, and the laws by which it moves are chemically and physically explained. In organic bodies, the process by which a being exists is totally different. The laws of Physics and Chemistry can indeed be transposed onto an organic being, but these sciences cannot disclose the nature of the process. The organic process takes place in a living body, obeying the laws of life, and reveals itself with clear and distinct signs, but its innate quality is very difficult to examine thoroughly or to understand—even though it is clearly a different process from that of inorganic bodies.

Thus, it is characteristic of and unique to organic bodies to produce signs of life in time and space. Such phenomena imply energies within organic bodies that are lacking in the inorganic.

The connection between these energies is the vital force [*vis vitalis*] by means of which the organism comes into being, is nourished and sustained. Through this resource, the organic body is capable, not only of preserving itself and guarding against external encroachments, but also of propagating the species and creating beings similar to itself. In short, the organic body reproduces itself not only internally but also externally. Internal reproduction is seen in the act of nutrition and involves a series of functions that are simpler in less advanced organic bodies than in those that are more advanced and closer to human nature.[15] External reproduction is seen in the act of generation, which obeys the same laws as nutrition: in lower beings it is simpler, and in higher beings, more advanced. Generation in organic beings is carried out by specific organs whose form corresponds to the level of perfection of the organic beings themselves. In the system of generation for lower beings, organic life [*vita plastica*] prevails.[16] In higher beings, animal life becomes visible later and in gradual stages. First among organic entities are the vegetative. More attention has been paid to their system of generation, and, indeed, Linnaeus's method of describing plants is based on the evolution of the genital parts. Although I assume that every reader must know about such things, I will, nevertheless, say a few words about the anatomical structure of this system in plants for the sake of improved clarity and to begin with a more simple topic.[a]

Any form of reproduction requires a polarity or, rather, a material and dynamic opposition that in higher animals manifests itself as sexual difference. But in lower beings it is indicated by

---

a. Here I venture to point out a path that a schoolteacher ought to follow if he wishes to steep his student in some idea about sexual function.

the different construction of the genitals. In plants, the organs of propagation divide into those that provide the seed of generation (semen) and those that take up this seed for the subsequent development of the embryo. The first pertains to the male genitals, the second to the female.

Male genitals consist of the stamen (the organ aiding the preparation of the semen); the anther (the organ analogous to the testes) that contains small cells filled with an oily substance similar to wax; and pollen (analogous to semen).

The female genitals consist of the ovary (a receptacle that later becomes the uterus in plants), a cellular body containing little water-filled cells (the Graafian vesicles) that after conception are transformed into seed.[17] The stylus (analogous to the vagina) is a column either hollow or solid that is joined to the ovary by means of vessels. If it is hollow, the channel does not lead into the ovary but is closed at the base (analogous to the opening of the uterus). The stigma (an organ analogous to the clitoris) is a cellular structure with prominent papillae, or fibers. Conception occurs through the sprinkling of pollen grains on the stigma, which, in a kind of arousal, excites considerable swelling and a growing vital force in the ovary. The pollen cannot actually reach the ovary because a connection is lacking between the stylus and the ovary, and on account of its unique structure, the stigma prevents the passage of the pollen.[b]

The eminent Linnaeus excellently divided plants into two groups according to the structure of their sexual organs: those with visible genitals,[18] the Phanerogama, which are the more highly evolved

---

b. Here would be the place to discuss the development of the embryo. Nevertheless, I omit everything pertaining to this in order to hold myself to what I have proposed—solely to explain aberrations in sexual function.

plants that are either monocotyledons or dicotyledons and are especially vascular,[c][19] and those with hidden genitals, the Cryptogamia, which are cellular acotyledons. The first group comprises twenty-three Linnaean classes; the second, a single and unique class—that is, a twenty-fourth class.

Phanerogama[20] divide into (1) the Monoclinia, in which sexual polarity is not apparent. Because each individual plant of this class enjoys both male and female sexual organs, hermaphroditism is manifest in each plant; and (2) the Diclinia, in which there is evident sexual polarity (*geschlechtlicher Gegensatz*) and that contains plants of different sexes. Monoclinia further divides into (1) "unmarried" plants, in which a certain kind of polarity exists between the andreceum (stamen) and gyneceum (carpel), and (2) "married" plants, in which this polarity is concealed by the unification of male and female sexual organs.[21] This union can be a stamen in a single bundle: Monadelphia (the sixteenth class); or in two: Diadelphia (the seventeenth class); or more: Polyadelphia (the eighteenth class); or in a unification of anthers: Syngenesia (the nineteenth class), or of the whole male and female systems: Gynandria (the twentieth class).[22] Among "married" plants, the relation to the sexual system is most manifest in the class Syngenesia, in whose forms there remains a certain difference between flowers of the *radius* and *discus*. The classes Monadelphia, Diadelphia, and Polyadelphia enjoy a lesser degree of development, while Gynandria is the least developed of all.

---

c. The cotyledon is the nucleus of the embryo (the seminal *lobus*). Whether it is absent or 1–2 are present, Jussieu divided plants into cellular plants that lack ducts and in which nutrition occurs through endosmosis and exosmosis and vascular plants that have vessels by which the distribution of fluid occurs. Vascular plants resemble animals, while cellular plants resemble minerals.

"Unmarried" plants are divided into the indifferent (the first thirteen classes) in which the stamens are of indeterminate length and the subordinate (the fourteenth and fifteenth classes) in which a certain difference is seen in the length of individual stamens. Subordinate plants encompass two classes: (1) Didynamia (fourteenth) with four stamens, of which two are longer; and (2) Tetradynamia (fifteenth) with six stamens, of which four are longer and two shorter. Among "unmarried" plants, the subordinate occupy a higher level of development relative to the sexual system and more closely resemble Diclinia than do indifferent plants. This is because in the subordinate plants a certain type of sexual polarity exists in the difference in the length of stamens. Diclinia encompasses three classes that exhibit sexual polarity in the following ways: (1) Monoecia (the twenty-first class), for which sexual difference exhibits in the individual flower, so that in one and the same plant the male genital system and the female genital system exist in different flowers; (2) Dioecia (the twenty-second class), for which sexual polarity is clear in the entire plant and it has a visibly distinct sex, so that one plant contains the andreceum and another the gyneceum; and, finally, (3) Polygamia (the twenty-third and final class of Diclinia), a combination of Monoecia, Dioecia, and Monoclinia, in which a distinct sex is able to be seen in one or in multiple plants, or there is clear hermaphroditism in the union of parts. This final class is easily explained. Nature does not make leaps; just as the plant and animal kingdoms are not sharply separated but rather united by means of Phytozoa and Zoophytes, likewise Polygamia unites Monoclina with Diclinia. In this class, nature has not yet rejected hermaphroditism but nevertheless attempts a more noble organization. Relative to the sexual system, Diclinia certainly is extremely developed and, to this extent, more closely approaches animal nature.

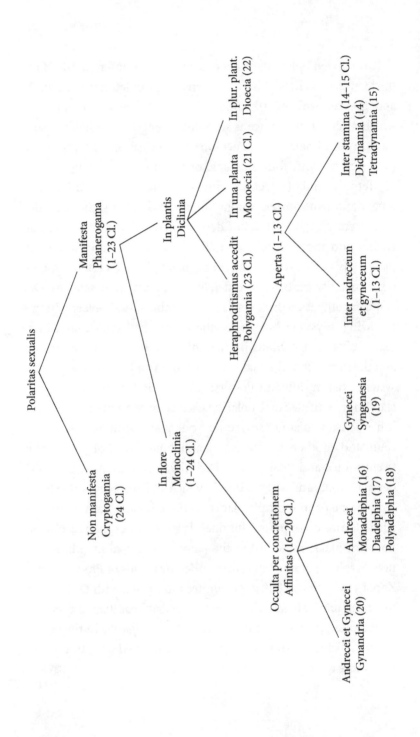

Developmental scale of the sexual system

Polarity not manifest . . . . Cryptogamia
Polarity is evident but hidden through joining of parts:
Union of the female and male genitals . . . . Gynandria
Union of the male genitals . . . . Monadelphia

Certain polarity in the fascicules . . . . $\left\{\begin{array}{l}\text{Diadelphia}\\\text{Polyadelphia}\end{array}\right.$

Union of the female genitals . . . . Syngenesia

Open polarity between the male and female genitals . . . . . . $\left\{\begin{array}{l}\text{Monandria}\\\text{Diandria}\\\text{Triandria}\\\text{Tetrandria}\\\text{Pentandria}\\\text{Hexandria}\\\text{Heptandria}\\\text{Octandria}\\\text{Enneandria}\\\text{Decandria}\\\text{Icosandria}\\\text{Polyandria}\end{array}\right.$

Between the male and female—distinction between stamen . $\left\{\begin{array}{l}\text{Didynamia}\\\text{Tetradynamia}\end{array}\right.$

Transitional class between Monoclina and Diclinia . . . . Polygamia
Polarity manifest in one plant . . . . Monoecia
    "   " in different plants . . . . Dioecia

Development of the Sexual System in Animals

The vegetable kingdom is not sharply separated from the animal kingdom. One moves into the other. There are closely related forms, and it is difficult to establish the definite signs that differentiate plants and animals. Indeed, traces of animal life may even be found in higher plants. In lower animals, however, this life force is not apparent through clear or distinct signs. Given that I never applied myself particularly to the study of Zoology, I must confess that everything I have deeply absorbed in regard to the development of this function in the animal kingdom comes from the *Zoologia specialis* of Professor Eduard Eichwald.[d][23] I cannot recommend the study of this book highly enough to all instructors and teachers for the purpose that I noted in the section on Therapy. I will attempt to describe, in a few words, Eichwald's classification.

The celebrated Eichwald names that raw and indistinguishable mass—"heaped together, the discordant seeds of badly joined matter"[24]—"Chaos" (what others call protoplasm) as either animal, if it provides the source for the unique development of animalcules, or vegetable, if it provides a source for plants' lower development. This Chaos is not a proper class but, rather, a primitive, almost elementary organization that exists as a passage into the animal kingdom (if it is animal) and (if vegetable) into the vegetable kingdom.

All sex differentiation is denied to the chaotic organization.[e] Indeed, an animal character may be distinguished only because the vesicles emit globules in every direction. These globules immediately begin increasing in circumference and then burst open once more, spilling forth new globules. These new globules that come out of the burst vesicles either immediately show the very same form, or, as they grow, they preserve their form such that there is absolutely no development of individual parts of the corpuscle. These chaotic vesicles should be grouped with the spores of the lower plants, especially of algae. Previously, writers of great and widespread reputation have observed that mucosal spores are produced out of algae. After having enjoyed free movement for a fixed time, these spores then turn into other algae, but of the

d. Dr. Eichwald, *Zoologia specialis*. Vilna, at the press of Joseph Zawoisky.
e. Vol. 1., sect. 9, p. 148; sect. 12, p. 151.

same species. Thus, a certain kind of reproduction through spores is suitable to the chaotic organization, and if we were to assign it a place in the previously discussed Linnaean system of plants, we would place it in the twenty-fourth class of Cryptogamia, for sexual polarity is not visible in the chaotic organization. The lowest animal classes according to Eichwald are the Phytozoa, which are close to a vegetative form (φυτόν plant, ζῶον animal) and which demonstrate a conspicuous affinity with vegetative plants; that is why every property of vegetative life is seen in these classes.[f]

The sexual reproduction of Phytozoa[g] comes from buds that arise sometimes individually or grouped together in fixed places on the body so that all its resources do not overburden its uniform multiplication. In this class, the sexual system is in a fixed location, bound to a certain area of the body. Thus, its differentiation is already distinct within its organic mass, in particular with respect to its generative faculty, and this differentiation is clear in the parts of the body from which the buds develop (as with vegetative plants in the crux of branches, so in specific places for Phytozoa as well).

Analogous with the Linnaean system, sexual polarity is clear in these organisms, and, consequently, in single individuals visible hermaphroditism is not evident but is hidden in its material composition. Eichwald divides Phytozoa into (1) monohyla, whose body is a homogenous mass that excels in free movement and is endowed with tiny hairs or tentacles; and (2) heterohyla, whose body[h] is formed from various substances. Either from a single part or from the whole, an animal gelatin is transformed into a non-contractile mass (the root of the heterohyla); the other animal part

f. Vol. 1, p. 158.
g. Vol. 1, section 21, p. 102.
h. Vol. 1, p. 172.

produces polyps, often without locomotion. Although authorities disagree concerning the relationship of polyps to the root, in the heterohyla I am able to discern a much higher development of the sexual system. In monohyla, no difference of mass distinguishes the organs of those endowed with the generative faculty and those that lack it. But in heterohyla the material difference is clear between the root and the polyps; thus, heterohyla absolutely occupy a higher level on the scale of development of the sexual system.

In the Linnaean system, monohyla seem to me to be comparable with gynandria, and heterohyla comparable with syngenesia on account of the differentiation between root and polyps (as with *radius* and *discus*).

The second class according to Eichwald is the Cyclozoa (κύκλος circle, ζῶον animal), in which a circular development of the body prevails. These animals are endowed only with female genitals[i]—that is, with an internal ovary that carries buds grouped together, or small eggs. One might exempt Holothuria from this class, as it manifests animal development to such an extent that it is possible to find some traces of masculine genitals. In Cyclozoa the polarity in the sexual system is more developed. Its female genitalia become conspicuous, and generation now takes place through eggs. In terms of male genitalia, they must exist in this class, for no reproduction happens without these in the higher orders (as in Holothuria); no one doubts this. But the organization of these is less developed or, at any rate, is less obvious to the eye. At this point I believe it is possible without risk to affirm that sexual differentiation is present in individuals of the Cyclozoa but that it is hidden by the material makeup of the muscles (or at least is not evident in the lesser members [of the class]). In the Linnaean system, I would

i. Vol. 1, p. 214.

assign these to Monadelphia, Diadelphia, or Polyadelphia, but to which of these three classes I would not venture to say.

The third class, according to Eichwald, is Grammozoa (γραμμή line, ζῶον animal), which is typified by the longitudinal linear dimension of the body. Growth takes place principally along the length of the body, mostly in the form of rings, and, on account of this strong dimension, one part of the body is set against another part without a break—in one part a mouth develops and in another the anus. But because the anus and mouth stand at opposite ends of the body, from the beginning division enters into the simple body, and consequently many rings form the body with each ring more or less uniquely separate. If a segment is released from the remaining body, it is able to live—in fact, it is able to develop into a new individual. This class displays great variety in its sexual organs, for the lowest [of the class] (Cryptogamia) clearly seem to lack these, while in others there are only the feminine genital parts (in Monadelphia, Diadelphia, and Polyadelphia), while in yet others the masculine parts are joined with the feminine (in Monoclinia), and in individual others a divided sex occurs (in Dioecia). It would be difficult to assign this class a place in the Linnaean system, seeing as the most diverse forms of the sexual organs occur in it; hermaphroditism also is present and even distinct sexes appear. A certain analogy is possible with the Polygamia of Linnaeus, which is truly a transitional class that unites Cryptogamia and Phanerogama or even the name Lesser Polygamia might be appropriate.

According to Eichwald, Therozoa (θήρ animal, ζῶον animal) occupies the fourth class because of its strong centripetal animal life (by contrast with Phytozoa, in which the animal life is centrifugal). In this class the lower animals have only feminine genital parts, ovaries, whose eggs are developed in a way similar to buds

(Monadelphia, Diadelphia, Polyadelphia). In others, there is her-maphroditism, either in a single individual (the undifferentiated Linnaean classes, 1–13) or with a distinct sex in a mutual bond (Monoecia) or between separated individuals (Dioecia). This class also cannot assume any particular place in the Linnaean system but is transitional and demonstrates the transition from her-maphroditism to distinct sexes. Here again the name "Polygamia" is merited, but a Polygamia of another order since Cryptogamia does not widely appear in this class.

Podozoa, the fifth class of Eichwald (ποῦς foot, ζῶον animal), enjoys distinct sexes, if you exempt certain orders of the crus-taceans (Entomostraca) and insects (Vespae, Apes, Formicae), which are considered to be lacking sexual differentiation and should be called "feminine," having genitals that are not com-pletely developed.[j]

In Spondylozoa, the final class (σπόνδυλος vertebra, ζῶον ani-mal), if you make an exception for certain genera of fish in which only the female exists, distinct sexes are present.

As the entire genital system offers a ladder of development, if you consider the polarity occurring in the entire animal and veg-etable kingdoms, just so even its shape or structure displays in-numerable mutations. In the lower classes, the simplest genital structure is found, but as an organism assumes a higher place in the scale of polarity, correspondingly it is more complex and com-plete, and therefore it more closely approaches the genital system in mankind.

j. Eichwald, vol. II, p. 165.

Developmental Scale

Scala evolutionis
Polaritas sexualis non manifesta.
Transitus a Cryptogamia ad Phanerogama.
Polaritas sex. occulta per concretionem.
  Concretio masculin. solum femineae partes.
Transitus ab hermaphroditismo ad sexum sejunctum
Polaritas sexualis qua sexus sejunctus.

Chaos
Grammozoa
Phytozoa
Cyclozoa
Therozoa
Podozoa et Spondylozoa
Polaritas Sexualis

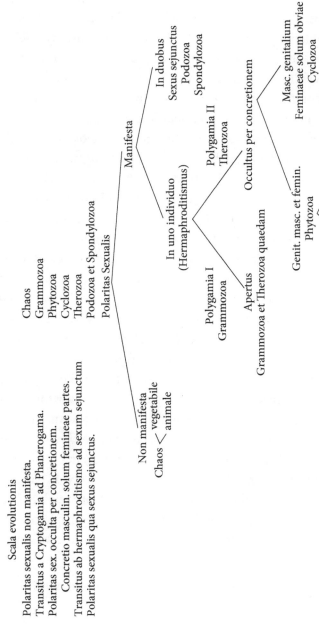

Non manifesta
Chaos ⟨ vegetabile
        animale

Manifesta

In uno individuo
(Hermaphroditismus)

In duobus
Sexus sejunctus
Podozoa
Spondylozoa

Polygamia I
Grammozoa

Polygamia II
Therozoa

Apertus
Grammozoa et Therozoa quaedam

Occultus per concretionem

Genit. masc. et femin.
Phytozoa

Masc. genitalium
Feminaeae solum obviae
Cyclozoa
Entomostraca
Apes, Formicae, pisces quidam.

Cum oppositione
Heterohyla

Absque oppositone
Monohyla

Traces of ovaries[k] can be found in certain of the microscopic
organisms, and they display a simple tube close to the abdominal
cavity containing eggs. In corals, the ovaries are already fascicu-
lated, and they produce not single eggs but ones joined together
with mucus. In mollusks, for the first time an ovary divided from
the mass of the body can be observed. In snails, the ovary divides
into a male part (ducts) and a female one (eggs). In segmented
worms, the configuration is multiform; in cystoids, the eggs are
separated into chambers by an internal wall. In ragworms and
lugworms, the ovaries lie like bladders behind the intestinal tube.
Tapeworms and liver-flukes are hermaphrodites, and wherever
their ovary is located, which sometimes terminates on the edge
and sometimes in a middle open area, there is also an opening
that leads to an exit canal (*Milchsack*). In parasitic worms, there
are two threads or canals; the ovaries are several cubits long, and
there are also two similar canals standing in for the masculine system. In many Helminthozoa (*Grammazoa interna*) a distinct sex
is present, although in completely developed worms (*Grammazoa externa*) hermaphroditism is found. In general, nature follows
no distinction between classes with respect to sexual polarity and
anatomical arrangement, and in any class whatsoever the lower
type is found that indicates the more superior type. An excellent
example is provided by Grammozoa and Thermozoa. For in the
former class, genitals are often lacking (Cryptogamia), while in
other members of the class small eggs sprout like buds (Gynandria); others display the feminine part alone (Monadelphia, Diadelphia, Polyadelphia), while for others there is hermaphroditism
in a single individual (Monoandria, Icosandria), in others a shared

k. Oken allgem., *Naturgeschichte für alle Stände*. In Stuttgart with C. Hoff-
mann, 1833, p. 447.

sexual bond (Monoecia), and finally a divided sex is found (Dioecia). In Thermozoa, we find the same thing except that a chaotic configuration (Cryptogamia) is lacking.

Let us pursue further the development of the sexual system's structure. In sea anemones, the ovaries—similar to tubes—move through the stomach and open up at the edge of the mouth. In polyps and sea cucumbers, there is a single tubular ovary with many branchings that open backward behind the mouth. Around the excretory ducts (a vestige of copulatory organs) lie eight or ten piriform corpuscles (masculine genitals). In sea urchins, five ovaries fill the space between the tube and shell; the glandula are yellow (analogous to mammals) and end at the anus (the genitals occupying a place of higher development). In lower-order animals, only the female genitals are found, while in the higher orders, only the male. But I do not believe the male genitals are, in fact, missing [in lower-order animals]. For there is no reproduction without sexual polarity, the traces of which can be seen even in the lowest orders. Perhaps the masculine genitals are not solid or are not fixed to a certain location and thus escape notice in an anatomical examination. For they certainly exist in lower-developed types, and it may be asserted that they are present even if the anatomical scalpel is not able to demonstrate them. Indeed, comparative anatomy does not enjoy a level of perfection such that it can explain the function of each and every internal organ in an animal specimen. For that reason, just because we do not see genitals does not prove that they do not exist. Daily we progress more in understanding the anatomical structure of different animals, and perhaps in the future what now hangs in doubt will become known. Therefore, I confirm that masculine genitals are always present, if sexual polarity announces itself in a certain place with clear signs, even when less developed and solid. They provide an analogy to Gynandria,

especially Monadelphia, Diadelphia, or Polyadelphia, which class
alone of all plants permits examination of the female genitals.

In insects the male organs (ducts) are clearly separated from
the female, and in all those that live in the air they terminate at
the posterior end of the body. In aquatic insects, wood lice, and
crayfish[1] all the genital organs, the ovaries and excretory ducts
alike, are doubled and (as the first doubling shows) terminate in
the middle of the abdomen, with a uniquely constructed opening
(the traces of a spherical genital orifice). In higher animals, without exception, there are ovaries and male genital organs, which for
the most part are doubled and in two separate individuals. In fish,
the ovaries and male genitals are two long tubes separated by an
internal wall; eggs and semen are emitted at the same time, and
they come into contact in the water. In amphibians, the ovaries
are two large clusters, and the oviduct is long, thin, and ends in
a cloaca; the male genital organs are two capillary sacks that receive many branches through a convoluted canal that looks like a
fleshy glandular mass (the first shape of human testes). The same
holds true for birds except that the two ovaries are hard and there
is one oviduct that is not perfectly shaped. In mammals, ovaries
are glandular and fleshy (as in the human woman) and terminate
in an empty germinal sack (an undeveloped uterus). From these
examples, the developmental scale of the sexual system for the
entire animal kingdom is made sufficiently clear, with mankind
occupying the first and highest place. For in mankind, not only
is sexual differentiation into male and female genitals completely
developed, which shows the greatest analogical parallelism,[25] but
the entire anatomical shape displays the pinnacle of refinement in
sexual differentiation. Even if I may assume anatomical knowledge

1. According to Oken, p. 455.

in my readers, nevertheless, a few words concerning the genital system in mankind are necessary. First, for the sake of completeness I dare not omit in my book a matter of such importance, and second, because in anatomical education a young man should not lack even this knowledge.

In both sexes, the genitals separate into reproductive organs or formative organs, in which the seed (*künftiger Bildungsstoff*) is generated and developed, and into the organs of copulation, which are primarily active in sexual union and contribute, not insignificantly, to the expulsion of seed. These latter are the organs intermediate between the external world and the sanctuary for the formation of an animate being (a human).[26] The reproductive organs enjoy the highest power. In them, organic life [*vita plastica*] achieves the acme of perfection, and animal life truly reaches the highest point of development through motion and sensibility.[27] Thus, these organs separate into those in which organic life[m] (a formative or reproductive impulse beyond itself) prevails and

Organs of generation in organic life

Organs of Generation:	in the male	in the female
	Testes	Ovaries

Organs of generation in higher organic life and animals

Vas deferens	Fallopian tubes
Seminal vesicles	
Prostate	Uterus
Cowper's Glands	

Organs of copulation

Male member	Vagina and clitoris
Ischiocavernosi muscles	Constrictores cunni
Scrotum	External labia pudenda

m. Czermack says, "*Blut ist Zeugungssamen und Samen ist Zeugungsblut.*" [Blood is the seed of procreation, and seed itself is procreation's blood.]

seed is generated and those in which organic life is raised up to a higher state of perfection. In this way, the seed is refined to a greater extent, and animal life, especially the power of motion, surges forth with the greatest force.

Sexual Organs of the Man[n]

The male sex contributes the preparation of fertilizing material for the reproductive act. The equipment serving this function consists of two separated glandules (testicles) and two canals (vas deferens) that collect semen from two cavities (seminal vesicles) that in turn retain it for the emission of this material out of the male member.

The testicles lie below the abdominal cavity in a special extension of the inner skin (scrotum), in the interior part of which a white membrane, the tunica dartos, forms an incomplete wall in the middle so that each testicle lies in its own cavity. A testicle is free and mobile, ovoid in shape, with one end tilted up and forward and the other end lower and inclined backward. Its coverings are: the albuginea, a fibrous bluish-white membrane that encircles it completely and tightly; and the tunica vaginalis of the testes, a membrane that in its normal state dispenses a serous secretion. The testicle itself is composed of intertwined veins carrying blood and canals carrying semen, which, after they perforate the albuginea, join together in a dense rope-like structure (epididymis), the upper part of which is called the head, the lower part the tail. In this, the semen-bearing tubes are joined and form a single main canal, the spermatic duct or vas deferens. The vas deferens (*zurückführendes Gefäss*) enters the abdominal cavity through the inguinal canal,

n. *Anthropologie*, by Carl Ernst von Baer. Königsberg, 1824.

arches toward the pelvic cavity, and runs under the bottom of the bladder where it approaches its counterpart. Veins and nerves also pass through the inguinal canal, which traverse from the abdominal cavity to the testicles. At the connection of these the spermatic cord arises. In this cord the vas deferens, the spermatic artery, vein, and nerve do not lie freely but rather are surrounded by a muscle layer (the cremaster) that encircles these structures as a sheath and greatly aids the testicle in descending at the moment of impregnation. Before the spermatic ducts approach each other and reach the mass of the prostate, each is joined with a reserve organ, the seminal vesicle (a gland composed of many lobes); this union happens at a sharp angle, and both terminate as a single ejaculatory duct in the urethra (in the caput gallinaginis) behind the mouth of its partner or in a shared opening.

The prostate is a solid body that encircles the neck of the bladder and the beginning of the urethra; many of the ejaculatory ducts empty into the urethra from both sides and pour out a mucosal material that is either mixed with semen or on its own leaves the body with a sense of pleasure.[o]

The male member, under whose root the Cowper's glands are found, is especially endowed for arousing the libido, with nerves arising from the spinal cord. It is comprised of three parts: (1) the corpora cavernosa of the penis (empty spaces that are visible in cross-section), two of which run together along the middle and form the primary mass of the penis; (2) fibrous membranes that encircle this and form almost a barrier down the middle; and (3) its parenchyma is erectile tissue. Therefore, under the incitement

---

o. For this reason onanism is so very dangerous; for not only does it cause the loss of semen but also a constant dripping of the prostatic flow and this is excited by the slightest pretext.

of the sexual instinct [*nisus sexualis*] a swelling of this organ (erection) occurs by an influx of blood, aided by the action of the ischiocavernosi muscles, which are known from this action as the supporting muscles of the penis. In the furrow formed through these two corpora cavernosa (penis) lies the urethra, which conducts the semen.[p]

The bulbo-cavernosus muscle (*Zellkörper der Ruthe*) surrounds the urethra as the accelerator of either urine or semen that through contraction especially brings on the emission of semen. The glans is also formed out of erectile tissue and is joined with the corpora cavernosa of the penis. The posterior margin of this (corona) swells, and a channel can be seen underneath it where a countless number of sebaceous glands can be discerned. This covering of the glans, something intermediate between skin and a mucosal membrane, after the edge of the glans turns itself, it forms the internal surface of the foreskin (*Vorhaut*). Because the corona of the glans is not circular, the foreskin at this point forms a fold of the glans.

---

p. Bock *Anatomie*: "die männliche Harnröhre fängt am Blasenhalse mit der Blasenmündung an, dringt vor—und abwärts mitten durch die Prostata, wo sich der Samengang und der Ausführungsgang der Prostata und der Cowperischen Drüsen in ihr münden, beschreibt einen leichten nach unten convexen Bogen unter der Schambeinsfuge hinweg und legt sich an die untere Fläche des Penis, an welcher sie vorwärts und durch die Eichel läuft und sich auf ihr mit der Hautöffnung endigt; in ihrer Lage unter den Zellkörpern des Gliedes wird sie von einem eigenen Zellkörper, corpus cavernosum urethrae, umgeben, bildet eine starke Anschwellung, die Harnröhrenzwiebel, bulbus urethrae." [The male urethra begins at the neck of the bladder with its opening, penetrates down through the middle of the prostate, where the sperm duct and the excretory duct of the prostate and the Cowper's glands all discharge into it, follows a slight downward convex curve under the pubic symphysis, and adheres to the lower surface of the penis, on which it runs forward and through the glans and terminates with it at the opening of the skin; in its position in the cell bodies of the limb it is surrounded by a particular cell body, the corpus cavernosum urethrae, which forms a strong swelling, the urethral bulb, bulbus urethrae.]

If the foreskin cannot be retracted over the glans, sebum accumulates around the glans, and perhaps for this reason circumcision originated among oriental peoples.

Semen, a white fluid, very oily, consists of[q]

900	parts water
60	parts unique animal matter
30	parts calcium phosphate
10	parts sodium
1,000	

Semen is divided between the testicles and arrives in the seminal vesicles through the vas deferens, where it becomes more refined and thicker (as much through the absorption of liquid as the secretion of new moisture in this organ). It pours through the ejaculatory ducts into the urethra (its prostatic part), where prostate fluid is mixed in with it and it is further refined. Then, chiefly through the contraction of the accelerating muscles of the urethra, it is emitted via the penis.

Female Sexual Organs

These organs are contained in the pelvic cavity (contrary to how it is for the man, where the testicles and male member lie outside this cavity). They consist of two ovaries, two oviducts or Fallopian tubes, a uterus, a canal that leads outward (vagina), and those parts surrounding the external sexual opening. Some of these organs (the ovaries, tubes, and upper part of the uterus) are covered by the peritoneum (the covering of the abdominal organs). This membrane forms on either side two expansive folds that support

q. According to Vauquelin, *Ann. de Chimie*, vol. 9, p. 77.

the pelvic organs in the normal position, and part of these folds
at the side of the uterus are called the ligamenta lata of the uterus.
The ovaries lie on either side of the uterus on the posterior surface
of the peritoneal fold (ligamentum latum) and are connected to
the uterus by a round solid band (the ligamentum proprium of the
ovary). First, a serous membrane (part of the ligamentum latum)
covers the ovary, and under this the tunica albuginea encircles the
actual ovarian matter. The parenchyma (*Keimlager, stroma Baer*)
consists of a solid dense mass, reddish-brown, that is formed from
bundled fibers of cellular tissue and a dense vascular network. In
the parenchyma of a virgin, there are between twelve or fifteen
round, clear membranous cellular structures (vesicles, follicles, or
Graafian eggs). After fertilization, the cells rupture and the con-
tents pour out; the cavity is then filled with a yellowish-red mass
and the corpus luteum implants itself.[r] On the upper boundary
of the peritoneal fold (ligamentum latum) lie the Fallopian tubes
or tubes of the uterus, which are better termed oviducts, as they
conduct the material to be molded (the seed of the embryo) from
the ovary to the uterus. These organs are two hollow tubes, one
opening of which terminates in the abdominal cavity in fringe-like
tissue, while the second and narrower opening descends into the
uterus (the tubes encircle the ovaries with the help of the fringe-like
tissue). A mucous membrane covers all the female genital organs
except the ovary; this membrane in the external orifice is contigu-
ous with the skin and, through the urethra, with the urinary system (just as in a man there is a continuous covering of the urinary
and sexual systems).

The uterus (*Mutter, Fruchthalter*) is a visible pear-shaped body,
a muscular cavity that is located in the pelvic cavity between the

r. Even without intercourse, this can arise from *Psychopathia sexualis*.

urinary bladder and the intestinal rectum.[28] It lies partly in the
peritoneal fold and consists of the fundus (this is the very large
and convex upper part), the corpus (this part is longer in the middle and narrower toward the back), and the collum, or cervix, the
lower part of which extends into the vagina and creates the vaginal portion of the uterus. This extension ends with two labia and
forms the mouth of the os tincae,[29] the orifice or external mouth
of the uterus. To be more precise, this opening joins the vagina
with the neck of the uterus rather than with the vaginal portion
of the uterus. The tubes (oviducts) attach themselves to the side
edges, as do the ligamentum rotundum of the uterus (through the
inguinal canal to the pubic mound), the ligamentum latum, and
the ovarian ligament. The uterus's cavity is narrow and triangular
in shape with its apex toward the back. The canal of the neck of
the uterus begins with the internal orifice of the uterus (between
the body and neck of the uterus) and ends in the external orifice
of the uterus (between the vagina and vaginal portion of the
uterus). The parenchyma is fibrous and woven through with veins
and nerves (in a lesser amount, for otherwise the volumetric increase of the uterus during pregnancy would become most incred-
ibly painful). These fibers, which form a mass, are in fact muscle
fibers that are less apparent before conception but that develop
further during pregnancy. A whitish-red mucosal membrane covers the uterine cavity. It is thin and covered with villi. The uterine
nerves issue as much from the nervous system of organic life (the
sympathetic, etc.) as from that of animal life (the spinal cord).

The vagina is a cylindrical membranous canal that curves in the
direction of the small pelvis between the urinary bladder and intestinal rectum and then descends from the middle of the uterus's
neck (known as the laquear or fundus of the vagina) to the female
pudendum. The vagina terminates in a slight fold with differing

lengths (hymen), sometimes it is half-moon in shape, sometimes ring shaped and is located in the pelvis between the lower pudenda and below the urethral opening; after its rupture, myrtiform caruncles (notched lobes) are established.[30] The vagina is made up of a dense and elastic cellulose membrane, under which lies a spongy layer of veins (like the corpus cavernosum) and of a mucosal membrane that covers the vagina's cavity with an anterior and posterior column of ridges.

The vulva (cunnus, female pudendum) consists of the external labia majora and the interior labia minora, the clitoris, and the entry point of the vagina with the openings of both the vagina and the urethra.

The labia majora are two external extensions of the skin (*Hautwülste*) that form the cleft of the vulva and, through their anterior and posterior commissure,[31] cross over into each other. The labia connect in the lower commissure of the labial frenulum (from one to the other), before which lies the fossa navicularis.

The clitoris, which is similar to the penis, occupies a place at the upper part of the vulva below the anterior commissure of the labia. It consists of two corpora cavernosa and a gland, is covered over by a foreskin, and also boasts a frenulum. The internal labia, or labia minora, are two cutaneous folds formed from a mucosal genitourinary membrane; they extend into the base of the vulva's cleft and occupy the intermediate vestibulum. Each labium expands into two folds, the upper of which forms the foreskin and the lower the frenulum of the clitoris.

The vaginal vestibulum is the bottom of the vulva's cleft and ends above the clitoris, just below the posterior commisure and at the side of the nymphae (namely, the labia minora). Here, two openings display themselves to us. The upper (having a position below the gland of the clitoris) is the fleshy opening of the urethra;

the lower is the entrance or orifice of the vagina that in a virgin the vaginal screen or hymen closes off.

The breasts are secondary genital organs, acinous glands, that are displayed on the anterior surface of the chest as two hemispherical rounds each with an aureola and nipple (before the third and sixth ribs). These occur only on a mature woman and are not developed in men (who lack the cluster of glands or any place for the cellular channel of the milk-bearing ducts). These milk ducts, which are connected to the cluster-glands or milk-bearing cells, are joined together into twelve to twenty excretory ducts that appear in the breast's nipple.[s]

The ovary is an organ that is especially devoted to the generation or formation of new individuals. The Fallopian tubes convey the matter that is formed by conception into the uterus. The uterus is the organ where the new organism develops. The vagina is the organ that directs and conducts the penis and male semen during intercourse, and the fetus in childbirth. The external parts are the organ of sexual pleasure that display a state of stimulation before and after intercourse. This stimulation in the internal genitals and throughout the whole organism produces a state of increased activity.

The external genitals of the female allow for an easy entrance of the penis, but there are certain conditions that make this duty more difficult: (1) the presence of the hymeneal membrane; (2) the natural narrowness of the vagina; and (3) the engorgement of the erectile tissue that surrounds the vulva and vagina. These conditions especially occur at first intercourse, which can be attended with a significant amount of pain. The man must conquer

s. For a simpler explanation of these genitals I recommend the images in Bock (*Anatomischer Atlas*).

these difficulties, although these because of [her] reaction excite the man, stimulate and increase his passion. For this reason, once the penis is introduced it is better to hold it in place, as friction with the vaginal folds increases arousal. The powers of mankind are certainly equal to this task because of the relationship between the size of the penis and vagina, the expansion of the vaginal canal, and the secretion of mucous.

At the beginning, the woman[t] is more inactive. Then little by little she joins in the orgiastic lust of the man that increases further until the woman, as if in an ecstasy, is seized with convulsions. I remain silent about how the motions of this act motivates the ovaries and tubes, since it is possible only to conjecture as nothing certain is established. Only one thing is not widely disputed and is agreed on by every physiologist[u]—that the pleasure that a woman feels does not depend on contact with the semen emitted by the man but rather on the action of the organs themselves, and that in women one can never find an emission of semen—the fluid excreted by women is merely vaginal mucus. At this point I fall silent concerning the more profound discussions of a mystery that nature has concealed behind a veil difficult to lift, and I refer my readers to the vast literature[v] in this field.

On Puberty

In early childhood, man is a private and separate entity. No bonds of nature, as they relate to propagation, connect him with the rest of humanity. His death has no impact on life's shared

t. *Physiologie de l'homme* by N. P. Adelon.

u. *Encyclopädie die medicinischen Wissenschaften*, by Meissner, vol. 13, p. 271.

v. Spallanzani, Dumas and Prevost, Cruikshank, Vallisnieri, Santorini, Bertrandi, Home.

experience; but a period of life arrives when that scene changes. Entering into the society of human association, man turns out to be a reproductive being or a citizen of posterity, propagating his own family line. He is able to carry out this act, the act of reproduction, for which animals direct the entirety of their lives and through its fulfillment many butterflies breathe out their souls. The organs through which mankind is able to fulfill this duty are the genitals, and that time of life when their power is awakened and reveals itself through certain clear signs is called puberty (*mannbares Alter*). Coincident with this time of life, adolescence, and its reproductive capacity are the complete development of the genitals and the end of the body's growth in height. Since this time of life is already in a certain relationship with the disease that I intend to thoroughly describe in this book, it is necessary to discuss more fully this material, and, for the sake of clarity, I will describe separately the mental and physical development of man.

Puberty ends childhood and makes the transition to adulthood. It begins around the twelfth year in girls and the fourteenth in boys, at which age the Old Testament laws allow for marriage.

The onset of puberty varies according to

1. Sex—more quickly in girls than boys.
2. Climate—sooner in hot regions; in torrid climates, girls reach puberty at eight and nine, boys at twelve.
3. Way of Life—later in inhabitants of the countryside (J. J. Rousseau).
4. Nation—among the French, in the thirteenth and fourteenth year; among the Italians and Spanish in the twelfth year; among the inhabitants of Persia in year nine and ten; in Arabia, Algeria, and along the Malabar Coast in the eighth and ninth year.
5. Quantity and Quality of Nutrients—food that is plentiful, heat producing, and moist accelerates puberty.
6. Temperament—most quickly in the choleric type, later in the sanguine; most slowly in phlegmatics.[32]

7. Mental and moral developmental level of the nation—clearly in backward, rustic populations, to whom the light of culture and humanity has not yet reached, puberty begins most quickly, and women in these places reach puberty quickly and quickly age.[w]

8. Race (*Menschenrace*)[x][33]—the black race of mankind more quickly than the Caucasian, and the Mongoloid also more quickly than the Caucasian

Physico-Anatomical Development in the Young Male

Man at this age reaches the full shape of his limbs and entire body. Skin loses its pale color and softness, hair grows extensively, cellular tissue becomes more dense and firm, muscles develop more,[y] while facial appearance (*Physionomie*) and family resemblance become visible at this time and the young man acquires a unique expression: his eyes are lively and fiery.[z] The first beard

w. In Guinea, the menstrual flux is prematurely brought on through intercourse with immature girls. In Porto Real, the flux is excited among the Ethiopians through use of a pessary made from wood, which is filled with ants and inserted into the vagina; the itching aroused by these insects causes a flow of blood down to the genitals (*Coutumes et cerimon, relig.* de Picart. vol. 7, p. 229). Stimulating lotions and aromatics among the Egyptians and many peoples of Asia accelerate the menstrual flow (Ovington, *Voyage aux Indes*, vol. 2, p. 28). In overly quick development of puberty, there lurks a strong cause for disposing the sexual instinct [*nisus sexualis*] toward aberration, about which we will talk later.

x. *Histoire naturelle du genre humaine* by Virey.

y. For a chaste young man, the arm in particular offers the best anatomical preparation, in which we can see clearly the position of its muscles.

z. The eye, almost the soul of the body, deserves the highest attention from both doctors and teachers; for an eye that is sunk down, murky, lacking brightness, and surrounded with a bluish ring offers a sad prognosis concerning the sexual life of the man.

replaces childish down, and the young man becomes hairy (hairs appear around the genitals and under the armpits). The brain enlarges quite a bit, especially at the back and lower part, and the cerebellum similarly increases. Its density is increased and at the same time gives off an odor of sperm. The bones complete their growth in height; the muscles appear more ruddy; the larynx becomes larger, and the glottis wider and longer;[aa] even the jaw is more formed, and the wisdom teeth erupt. The genitals enjoy increased volume and ability so that they cannot help but fulfill their function. The testicles are twice as large and secrete semen. The penis is larger and able to have an erection. The scrotum acquires a darkish coloring. Even the breasts are partially involved in the development of the sexual system, for often in adolescent boys they swell and a milky substance pours out of them.

Physico-Anatomical Development in the Female

The female also achieves the full shape of her limbs and body at the age of puberty, but her entire constitution retains more traces of childhood. Her skin remains white; indeed, sometimes is even whiter. Differently than with men, fat joins together her muscles and thus the feminine form is more soft and round. In a woman, the lymphatic system predominates, and consequently her temperament is phlegmatic (physical) more often than sanguine. Women grow hair in the pubic region and armpits, and their genitals in particular reach a complete level of development. The ovaries grow twice as large; the uterus aids in the new secretion of blood,[34] the clitoris is covered over by hair; the labia extend

---

aa. From this comes the change in voice from high to low; a child sings with a high sharp voice *(Alt)*, a young man more often with a low voice *(Bass)*.

down; the pelvis increases in size; and the breasts[bb] attain their normal size.

Physico-Physiological Development in Both Sexes

With respect to the physical functions, a very extensive change occurs at the age of puberty. Although the animal functions are especially developed, and the motor and intellectual faculties equally attain a higher order of development, nevertheless all the vegetative functions also play a part in this development, and the output of their unique functions is also increased.[35] Digestion requires an ample food supply both for the growth of the body and for the energy expended by all the organs, which consume a greater amount [of energy] and require a more swift recovery.[cc] At the time of puberty new natural instincts are awakened that transfix the whole mind of both boys and girls, so that the appetite for food is lessened or is directed onto other matters and also those not relating to food (as in choleric girls). The ravenous appetite of boys is diminished; the adolescent thinks it beneath him to choose food and does not care much at all about his sustenance. Because the increase in body size and more complete development of all the organs comes about by way of the blood, those organs that produce blood ought to receive a greater share of vim and vigor. The larger stomach is able to digest a greater quantity of nutrients, and the lungs gradually increase so that a larger amount of blood

bb. Behold the fruit of today's education! So many young girls who lack breasts, the greatest attribute of physical beauty, wonder at their mothers, whether they themselves will be fit for giving milk, unmindful that at the age of puberty they will grow womanlike with respect to their genital system.

cc. From this, a common saying is *der Bube kann nie genug haben, er isst den ganzen Tag.* [The boy can't get enough; he eats the whole day.]

is produced and a sanguine temperament (physical) results. The more developed nutritive organs acquire a higher animal function; as a result, the muscles contain more fibers, the blood less serum and more globules, and the nervous tissue appears denser. Also, in excretion, we are able to observe a more animalistic nature: in the urine, ureum (*Harnstoff*)[dd] takes the place of the benzoic acid [found in the urine of] younger children; sweat emits a more acrid, aromatic odor similar to musk or amber.[ee] Every function of the organism enjoys vigor and power, which corresponds to the mental and moral state of puberty. The function of the genital system becomes awakened: in girls their regularly recurring menstrual flow and for a young man the secretion of sperm and frequent erections herald that each is capable of the procreative duty.

Psychological Development at the Age of Puberty

The new instinct that now appears is overcome by every external sense: sight and hearing become more acute, while the more animated quality of a young man's features expresses a daring attitude, a certain kind of mental and physical excitability. In a girl, it is expressed as modesty and excessive display of herself, but both sexes are preoccupied with the comb and the mirror. Their language is more vivacious. Almost every young man is a rhetor. He clings avidly to the impressions of external things, his imagination

dd. Ureum was detected in urine by Rouelle in 1773. It is the primary element in urine and an organic substance that contains much nitrogen.

ee. It is not a difficult task to distinguish by odor a functional man from one who is impotent. Julius Klaproth observed many eunuchs in his journey among the Tartars and Nogai. A eunuch's skin has wrinkles; his beard is sparse; he is a similar to a woman. In those places a law orders eunuchs to avoid men and seek out women; such individuals are called "chess" (without a beard).

fills up his intellectual function, his memory is tenacious, his judgment is marred and hasty, and his reason is less developed. Everything that is seen sharply strikes the young man's mind and sense, and he is aroused to take action by them. He seeks out something to occupy himself, but at every moment[ff] he changes his intention. Now the muses smile on him, and every man, at least at this moment, indulges himself in music. He loves dancing and plays the poet; a drive for creating and inventing appears. At this age, passions are awakened, and various moods of the soul shatter the youth. His entire animal function is more developed not only his emotive faculty but also that of movement. He is aware of the vigor of his motor faculty and is impelled to exercise it. He delights in war, travels, and hunting.

This new instinct exerts its power throughout the whole organism, and the highest moral and intellectual activity makes itself apparent. Not only does a new capacity emerge, but even—since all the faculties acquire a new level of excitement—the mind displays a great power and ability, and the soul, a feverish heat. The moral man through nature's rule is turned now to the blossoming of life. Aware of his strengths, he trusts in them and hopes for a fortunate outcome. A young man is at any rate foolish, silly, proud, arrogant, and inflated with a high opinion of himself, but at the same time he is imbued with generosity and magnanimity and has no knowledge of greed or jealousy. He is forgetful of his own interests. Such kind hopes offer themselves to the young man who is nobly trained with a boy's upbringing and learning! If we read the history of illustrious men, is it not possible to discover the traces of great intellect and splendid talent at this age of the young man?

ff. At that time, young men long to abandon Minerva and follow Mars, while many girls seek a cloistered life.

By how much did the greatest of men—Schiller, Goethe, Mozart, Haydn, Napoleon—excel at this age! Certainly, the future lot of those who at this life stage are lazy and ignorant will be grim and dubious.

On the Sexual Instinct

The instinct that commands all of life, both mental and physical, impresses its mark on all organs and symptoms; it begins at a specific age (puberty) and also ceases at a certain age—this is the sexual drive (*Geschlechtstrieb, Begattungstrieb*). For instance, there is an internal sense belonging to each function of the human organism that arises through contact with the external world, and this sense makes man aware of the vital state of each organ as [the feeling of] thirst, hunger, and fatigue. Likewise, the task of procreation enjoys its own unique instinct, an internal sense that makes man aware of the state of his genital organs and excites him to satisfy this instinct. Although this instinct may be recognized throughout the entire animal kingdom, it can be clearly demonstrated only in those animate beings in which the vital organs are situated on either side with a fixed symmetry and in which a cross-section displays nearly the same arrangement on both sides. Then a definite polarity rules not only over the sexual system but over the organism's entire organization. For these animals are accustomed to a doubleness of sense or to senses working in harmony, and in them there arises sympathy and antipathy or physical love and hate. Thus, in beings that enjoy distinct sexes, desire and mutual affection are required, since it is necessary for copulation, so that they mutually seek out each other and live in a state of joined union. Accordingly, both the entire external sensory system and the seat of these sympathies must be highly developed; thus, the sexual instinct manifests itself in definite signs at that time when they are driven by the passion of Venus. Although in certain (animate beings) lacking symmetry this instinct can be assumed, yet there are no definite signs of its presence. In lower-order animals, the procreative faculty makes its assault more swiftly, and, indeed, is faster relative to the greater simplicity of the body's constitution, that is by how much less developed is its animal function and how much more closely it approximates the nature of plants. In infusoria and polyps this activity appears after birth; in mollusks, in the third year of life; in fish, sooner than in amphibians; while in mammals the time to breeding varies widely.[36] First of all, the male is almost always found to be ready for intercourse later than the female. The most common time for the passion of Venus is spring, and especially in the months of March, April, and May; only predatory animals mate in winter. The time during which the passion for mating lasts varies; for example, in sheep it lasts for twenty-four hours; pheasant and black grouse (*Birkhuhn*) are driven mad for two months; males are always ready for coitus but females only at a certain time.

Throughout the entire animal kingdom the sexual instinct leads to copulation, and copulation (coitus) is the natural way by which a being satisfies the sexual instinct and performs life's duty, namely of preserving its own species.

There are various kinds of copulation:

Pantogamy:[37] indiscriminate Venus, in frogs, dogs, and wolves. Hence the Latin term *Lupa* (*Hure*).[38]
Polygamy: of which there are two types

Polygyny: multiple females with one male, as in some birds and mammals
Polyandry: multiple males with one female, as in bees and ants

Monogamy: which is temporary, lasting as long as the passion of
Venus does, as in dormice; or perpetual, as in foxes, eagles, doves,
the inseparable parrot, etc.

Copulation in animals varies widely with respect to the time of
day. Wood grouse, black grouse, and deer copulate in the morning.
Fish, bats, dragonflies, snakes, and lizards copulate in the middle
of the day. Gnats copulate at dusk. Worms, cats, moles, and others, after sunset. Animals entice one another to copulate in various
ways: with antennae and repeated contact, as in snails, or by striking one another as do fish and salamanders. Some animals, such as
the freshwater snail, are equipped with special organs. The rooster
repeatedly beats with his beak; the male cat bites. Many animals,
such as cats and lions, express their desirous feeling with a cry.
The female frog wails; the male tortoise emits a unique sound. The
female is passive during copulation and the male active, and in all
animals, one sees a momentary paralysis. With bugs and beetles,
nothing disturbs the act of copulation. Frogs remain joined if their
feet or indeed even their heads are cut off. Bats drop from the sky
as if they have fallen into sleep.

The duration of copulation varies. It is momentary among may-
flies, extremely brief among lizards, longer among ostriches and
swans. Among dogs, wolves, and foxes it lasts four hours. Certain
insects copulate over many days; frogs and toads for five to twenty
days. The bear incessantly repeats copulation. The rooster copu-
lates fifty times a day, the cow four to six times a day, and small
sparrows twelve to twenty times in a single hour.

Even though in man the sexual drive matures during puberty,
nevertheless its traces may be observed earlier, for in childhood
boys love manly pastimes and girls those of women; they do so
under the direction of their natural instinct. This sexual instinct

appears among children under the guise of a curiosity to explore
the functions of sexual life. Children eight or nine years old often
examine one another's genitals, and these explorations escape the
notice of parents and teachers.[gg]

At the moment when the first indication of sexual life appears,
a sense of modesty forms, which is something uniquely and es-
sentially human. It owes its origin neither to upbringing nor to the
society of mankind. It may be observed in people of a great variety
of types, in the uncultured as much as the civilized, the rustic as
much as the urban.

Having arrived at the stage of puberty, the youth is agitated by
a secret unrest; through his musings some mark of an uncertain
sensitivity is pressed into him. His soul is moved by gloomy feelings and delightful pleasure; he indulges in charming hope and
creates dreams for himself. Ordinary tasks are in themselves un-
satisfying, and the youth flees the company of people and seeks
solitude. On account of their more developed and active nervous
system, girls are especially tortured by this emotion of the soul.

At this time, an obscure desire erupts that dominates all the faculties of the mind and that the body's every strength obeys—the desire for love, that emotion and movement of the soul by which every
man is afflicted at least once in his life and the power of which may
certainly be denied by no one. The first effect of love's madness in-
spires the idea of chastity: a young man loves without sexual desire;
he willingly sacrifices his blood and life on behalf of his love; the
name of his beloved girl excites him, her presence stirs him up, he
feels her approach even from a distance, and the press of her hand
grazes him as if with electric sparks. Every thought of love for her is

---

gg. This matter is of the utmost importance, and a curiosity that is not satisfied
constitutes a decisive stage in the etiology of the disease, as I shall describe.

treated as sacred. By day, as her servant, he tries to fulfill the wishes and desires of his beloved already guessed at from afar, and at night his dreams present her image to him. A magnetic, true relationship arises between two people who love with shared souls, and indeed nothing is conceivable as more blessed than this period of first love, out of which flow so many examples of courage of a bold and generous soul. A young man enjoys this love, an adult man plucks the fruit, and an old man is amused by its recollection. The first leaning of the soul is therefore toward a moral love, and nature in this act demonstrates to us that man is a superior being. The soul holds sway, and the body is subject to its control—for the thought of fulfilling this lust would seem to bring harm to the very person to whom all our desires and prayers are dedicated. "First Love" performs what amounts to its own type of sacrificial rites: it offers its victim at the front of the temple, but does not dare to penetrate the hidden secrets of the temple. Even a strong and bold man, at that moment, is timid. Sensual pleasure once fulfilled brings an end to moral love. For this reason, a man rarely takes in matrimony a woman whom he has previously enjoyed. Thus, matrimony is necessary as a legal and religious bond, for otherwise a father might abandon his children and wife on account of his soul being estranged from them, and the basis of civilization, the family, would fall apart.

For this reason, almost every man owes his induction into a more refined state of humanity to this period of his life—or rather to the power of his most healthful love, whom he tries to please and for the benefit of whom he toils, devotes himself, and strives. How great a difference is there between the man who is filled with a chaste love and one who has satisfied his desires prematurely. The latter will always be licentious, devoted to bodily pleasure. His sexual instinct will rule throughout his life, and every higher sense of life and reason will remain uncharted territory to him.

A young man, therefore, does not seek at the first opportunity to satisfy his sexual instinct; even though there are many women "qui donnent la première leçon du plaisir amoureux" [who offer the first lesson in amorous pleasure], truly the young man hates these women and turns away.

Aristotle seeks for an explanation in the moral character of these women, who are mostly driven by lust, and, more advanced in age, snatch up a youth's first fruits.[39] From that point, the young man recognizes the shamefulness of the person who seduced him and harbors a loathing against her. An even more pertinent additional reason [for his loathing] is that the young man, with his incompletely developed body, fully recognizes the effect premature intercourse has had and he recoils from the person to whom is owed his state of infirmity. I am convinced without question that this kind of copulation between a beardless youth and an old woman lacks every sense of harmony: a young man neither thinks highly of such a person nor loves her. No wonder, then, that he spurns the woman who has destroyed all his dreams and enervated his bodily powers. The sexual instinct shows itself in a man who is endowed with reason and eloquence at first in the form of Socratic or Platonic love (*Platonische Liebe*), then over time he becomes more "Cynical"—but this occurs later in men than in women.[40] A woman yields against her will,[hh] and a man overcomes her obstacles and takes his pleasure. The nature of man presents a marvelously effective means for physical love under the form of repulsion. A girl flees a young man and hopes that he follows; she pretends to resist but desires to surrender; she hides her love and feigns that she hates the one whom she loves. Nevertheless, she is never more inspired by love than when she pretends to turn away.

hh. How greatly ought so many seducers be condemned, who abuse this law of nature!

These obstacles increase her love. With her eyes half-closed, she consecrates herself to her man and does not listen to the advice of her parents and others who try to dissuade her. She loves, and, trusting in that, she has no care for her future.[ll]

While man is able to perform intercourse at a specific time (in the morning on account of new energy acquired as a result of the preceding sleep, in midday as a result of nutrition, and at night with the help of the imagination), a woman is ready at any hour.[41] Hence, it is necessary for the man to solicit sexual pleasure, but the woman to reject him so as to amplify his desire.[jj]

The sexual instinct induces man to coitus, which human nature demands and which neither morality nor religion opposes; the propagation of the human race depends on this act. Nevertheless, among the various types of copulation, neither pantogamy nor polygamy are suitable for humankind—these types occur in the animal kingdom and exist among the primitive people of Africa and Asia,[kk] and to the shame of the human race some traces of these may be found in well-founded cities—but only monogamy, which leads to marriage, is suitable.

The laws of all nations urge marriage, and indeed, Genesis says (First Book of Moses, c. 2 v. 18): "The Lord God spoke: It is not right for man to be alone. I wish to make a helper for him, who will be with him." The brilliant Virey, in his history of the human race, adequately defended the absolute necessity for monogamy and marriage.[42] To this defense, I will briefly add a few arguments for marriage and against the state of celibacy, and also against pantogamy and polygamy.

ll. Marriages that love initiates are opposed to those that sexual desire or another reason have drawn together.

jj. Just as throughout the entire animal kingdom, the male solicits copulation and the female submits; only in the cat family does the female do the soliciting.

kk. The Ottoman Empire certainly deserves to be counted as part of Asia.

1. The structure of the human body is such that polygamy and pan-togamy are harmful types of copulation: seeing as one woman befits one man, and the period of menstruation, pregnancy, child-birth, and nursing is an interval necessary to the man's recovery.
2. Who does not see the great moral differences between celibacy and marriage?
3. The decline of states stands in direct relation to the increase in celibacy.
4. Without marriage there is no family, and the nation ought to be made up of families.
5. Men seek marriage in poor regions where morals are not cor-rupted, yet they flee from it wherever excess rules and a life of luxury holds sway.
6. Marriage is the best prophylactic remedy against an aberration in the sexual instinct, which we will discuss later.
7. The religious worship of all nations encourages marriage.
8. The more primitive a people and the less cultivated their intel-lectual abilities, the more a promiscuous Venus reigns.
9. Today's youth offer a sad example of the violation of nature's law, which enjoins marriage.

The sexual drive (pleasure, if it is satisfied; a punishment, if it is rejected) admits innumerable variations, if you consider the greater or lesser satisfaction of this desire. As regards quantity, it may be amplified or diminished:

1. According to sex: more amplified in women less in men.
2. According to temperament: it prevails among the sanguine and the choleric, less among the melancholic, and least of all among the phlegmatic.
3. According to constitution: a more powerful nervous system and the premature development of the genitals amplify the sexual instinct—at least for a while.
4. According to advanced diseases: all diseases whose onset is ac-companied by an excitement of the nervous system or its dis-turbance amplify sexual appetite (mental illnesses, epilepsy,

hysteria, phthisis, etc.). On the contrary, diseases accompanied by a torpor of animal and vegetable life nearly extinguish the sexual drive (melancholy, constipation, etc.).

5. According to nutrition: it delights most vigorously among cannibals, less so among carnivores and fish eaters, and least of all among vegetarians.
6. According to the time of year: more in spring and summer, less in winter. Indeed, Buffon demonstrates that the heat of summer contributes to fecundity;[43] the months when the sexual instinct boils up are July, May, and August. October, March, and April on the contrary.[ll]
7. According to climate: more in hot regions, less in temperate regions, and least in the northern regions. But [people in warm climates] both mature and grow old more quickly.
8. According to race: most in Ethiopians, less in the Mongoloid lineage, and least in the Caucasian.
9. According to way of life: more in the hard-working farmer than in the sedentary city dweller.
10. According to habit: moderate exercise arouses the sexual instinct and amplifies the capacity for procreation. Too much extends the sexual drive for a period, that is then followed closely by this system's complete listlessness, a complex infirmity. Absence of all exercise causes simple infirmity and removes the capacity for procreation.

Intercourse is recommended for men twice a week.[mm] According to Muhammad, once in eight days; according to Zoroaster, once in ten; and according to Solon, once in eleven.[44] Hence, we see that the laws of all nations ban and forbid too much coitus.

ll. Stein, *Causae sterilitatis,* 58. Wargentin, acad. vol. 16 from 1734 and vol. 18 from 1757. Act. Helvet. vol. 6. Buffon Suppl. vol. 2 in 4. Rabelais, *Pantagruel,* bk. 7, chap. 20.

mm. And a German proverb says: *in der Woche zwier, schadet weder mir noch dir.* [Twice a week harms neither me nor you.]

The age at which coitus may be performed has been designated by law: thus among the German people, according to Julius Caesar, a certain law forbade the exercise of the sexual drive before the twentieth year. And the energy and tall stature of the Teutons was most justly attributed to this.

Just as the sexual drive (*Geschlechtstrieb*) displays numerous variations with respect to quantity, likewise it also deviates from a standard norm with respect to quality; and different means exist for satisfying the sexual instinct and effecting coitus. The types of these aberrations are numerous enough, but the most common are onanism or masturbation, the love of boys (παιδεραστία), lesbian love, the violation of cadavers, sex with animals, and the satisfaction of lust with statues.

Onanism, or masturbation, is the fulfillment of the sexual drive by means of the hand. It is encountered among animals, for example, as in the male elephant who grips his penis between his hind legs and stirs up the evacuation of semen. M. Geoffroy observed (Ann. mus. vol. 7, p. 227) the fruit bat (of Brisson) lick its penis for this reason.[45] Monkeys are extremely given to this vice, especially those species that enjoy the use of hands, breasts, and a free penis (Virey, p. 41).

Onanism occurs in the Old Testament (II. Moses c. 38, v. 6, 7, 8, 9), and traces of it may be found throughout history.[46] It has quickly advanced along with human and civil culture; nevertheless, it is regularly encountered among uncivilized peoples, especially in America.[nn]

---

nn. Lopez de Gamora, *Hist.* bk. 2, chap. 1, and bk. 3, chap. 13. Steller Kamtsch, 287. Garcilasso de Vega, *Hist. des Incas,* bk. 2. Lamotraie vol. 2, chap. 3. Charlevoix, *Nouv. Fr.* bk. 2, p. 4. Dumont: *Louisiana.* Among Greeks and Romans: Philippus Camerarius, Horae subsec. cent. 2, chap. 46.

Pederasty is the manner of consummating the sexual instinct with immature boys. Its signs[oo] are redness, a burning pain around the anus, traces of discharged blood, tenesmus, difficulty walking, condylomata, hemorrhoids, inflammation of the anus and rectum, ruptured perineum, fistulae, prolapse of the rectum, and enervation of the rectum and the urinary bladder. The civil code of all nations severely punishes this vice either with incarceration, permanent exile, or death (among the English).

Lesbian love is an aberration that consists in the satisfaction of the sexual drive either between men or between women by means of tribadism, or rubbing.[47]

According to Ovid,[pp] Orpheus was the originator of this abominable vice:

> He was the first of the Thracian people
> to transfer his love to tender boys and this side of youth
> to pluck their age's brief spring and first flowers.[48]

Moreover, it is known how old this aberration is in the Orient. Even among Muhammad's polygamous followers, women in the female quarters are tribades, and the Turks punish this vice. It also occurs among uncivilized peoples, such as the Cacta in North America.[qq]

Even the violation of cadavers occurs.[rr] The signs of it are when the cadaver's limbs exhibit a change of position: the knees bent, legs spread apart, and the external genitalia enlarged; in virgins, the signs are a recently broken hymen and traces of semen in and around the vagina.

oo. Bernt, *Medicina legalis*, 100.

pp. *Metamorph.* 10.85.

qq. Bossu, *Nouv. voyages aux Indes occid.*, vol. 2, p. 100.

rr. Haller, *praelectiones* sect. 42, p. 301—tells of a girl who appeared to be dead, but was fertilized.

Intercourse with animals is certainly more difficult to detect. Suspicion first arises if the animal is discovered to be wounded around the genitals.[ss] The inhabitants of Persia who are afflicted with hip pain are said to give themselves over to this vice as a remedy.[tt] Driven by superstition, Kamchatkan women excite male animals to sex.[uu] Leviticus makes mention of coitus with beasts and prohibits this for Jewish women.[vv] [49]

The inhabitants of the island of Madagascar live like animals. Boys and girls engage their lusts in the presence of their parents, who laugh. Boys exercise their sexual appetites with animals. Moreover, even slaves commit illicit sex with cows and go unpunished. Also found on the island are the Tsecats, impotent and effeminate men who seek out boys with whom to indulge their lust but repel women and do not enjoy sex with them.[ww] Among the ancients, several examples of intercourse with animals are found. The women of Mendesia had sex with a sacred bull,[xx] and this act was often performed in front of everyone.[yy] [50] In the age of Trajan and Hadrian, a great number of beautiful women surrendered themselves to pleasures with a sacred animal, but the bull greatly preferred his own female, hating this detestable intercourse.[51] According to Diodorus Siculus, pious and religious women offered themselves naked and in the pose of venereal passion:

ss. J. Warton, *Note on Theocrite idyll I*, vol. 88, p. 19. Sicilian goatherds with goats and the holy Saracen (274) with a little donkey. Baumgarten, *peregrin. in Aegypt. Arab.*, 73.—

tt. Pallas, *neue nordische Beiträge*, part 2, p. 38.

uu. Steller, *Beschreibung von Kamtschatka*, 289.

vv. Chap. 17, 19, 20.

ww. Flacourt, *Madagascar*, 86.

xx. Hancarville, *Recherches sur l'origine des arts de la Grece*.

yy. Herodotus, 2.46.

.... at Mendes,
Where a she-goat's lecherous husband
Dares to penetrate a human female[52]

Men allowed themselves similar pleasure with goats. From this the worship of Pan and such honors for his priests were decreed. This religious superstition existed before Moses,[zz] and women of the Jews used to dance naked in front of the bull of Adonai,[aaa] and this continued to take place in the second century AD. Such scenes can be seen in the sculpted works of the ancient Greeks.[bbb][53]

All these most miserable types of aberration of the sexual drive deserve contempt and avoidance by which they may be overturned. For as with the laws of nature, so too the civil code and church teaching all condemn these aberrations and punish them in their followers. Even among uncivilized peoples, various remedies are attempted to guard against onanism: rings in the labia of the vagina,[ccc] bells on the male member.[ddd] On the island of Zubut, the rings are made of gold; in Turkey, of iron (Nicolai). Labillardière relates that in the southern islands there are certain mollusks that are suspended in the same place such as the shell of the *bulla ovum*.[eee]

What Is *Psychopathia Sexualis*?

How does it come to pass that a man instructed and refined by a liberal education succumbs to a vice whose shamefulness even

zz. Leviticus 18:7.
aaa. Berhard Hierozoic, pp. 643 and 842.
bbb. The collection from Herculaneum and Pompeii presents a series of obscenities.
ccc. Pierre de Saintré, *Voyage en Guin. I.*
ddd. Odoardo Barbari.
eee. Pigafetta *Congo* 2.

savages recognize, which reason forbids, and laws condemn and
punish severely? The cause cannot depend on external circumstances, for this vice occurs among all peoples, in far-flung regions,
at various times of life, from furthest antiquity up to the present
day, in the most different of life's stations. Very few are the men who
are found to be entirely immune from this disease. This cause is
not located outside of us but within us; it is a diseased imagination
that creates a premature sexual desire and seeks means and paths
for consummating the sexual drive. Once it is fulfilled in a manner other than the natural one, our nature becomes accustomed
to this method, which, repeated under the stimuli of a libidinous
imagination, becomes a firm habit. This immoral habit wields an
amazing power over man; neither a very strong will nor reason
itself are able to liberate him from it. Therefore, in every distortion
of the sexual instinct, it is the imagination that supplies the path
that fulfills it, contrary to the laws of nature. All these types of deviation are merely different forms of one and the same thing, and
they cross into one another. Boys who are given to onanism, even
if dissuaded from this habit at a later age, most easily fall into other
aberrations of the sexual drive; and among primitive peoples, one
type occurs at the same time with others. Thus, in every case of
sexual aberration a morbidly aroused imagination holds sway,
which clouds the mind.[54] It seems to me neither absurd nor false
if I collect all such states together as a disease of the imagination
that emanates from the sexual system and reflects back on itself
and under a single term, *Psychopathia sexualis*, understood in the
broadest sense. *Psychopathia sexualis* in the narrowest sense even
presents itself among adults in whom sexual life enjoys normal
vigor: it betrays itself in the form of a deliberately willed arousal of
the imagination and through the sexual system. There are, indeed,

countless incitements that, in accord with the unique constitution of each soul (ἰδιοσυνκρασία), inflame the imagination, excite the sexual instinct, and bring about intercourse.[fff] This disease is the state that others unjustly have called mental Onanism and regarding which I have gathered some text cases. However, I have it in mind to discuss these more extensively in another place.

Given that onanism occurs frequently and the opportunity to observe it lies open to everyone, I have specifically treated it in this little work as the most common and widespread form of *Psychopathia sexualis*. Those things that are said about masturbation bear on the other sexual aberrations, since what is said about the species pertains as well to the genus.

Now follows Onanism as a species of *Psychopathia sexualis, pars pro toto*: its etiology, diagnosis, effects on the human organism, prognosis, and therapy. To this I have added the diseases that follow as a consequence.

---

fff. The imagination's delusions are astounding. A beautiful foot holds for some the stimulus to pleasure, for others a hand, others breasts, yet others teeth; indeed, even clothing and belts can act on a man in a peculiar way.

Part 2

A lthough it would be of the greatest value for a more straight-forward survey to distinguish structuring causes from those that are accidental, this is rather difficult to do, as no structuring cause can be found that prepares the child for immodesty and places in it the seed of lust that does not also suffice for giving rise to masturbation.[1] For at that time when emotional life is heightened, which according to the laws of development is most influential in children, if, by chance through some impulsive stimulation of either the imagination or the genital sphere the feeling of sexual lust is aroused, sexual life becomes a focus for the person's entire life, and the child is driven to act even against its will. Regardless, for the sake of clarity, we will attempt to study those causes that predispose [a person to the psychopathy] and those that are accidental.

The disposition that supports the generation of this vice, is either:

A. Hereditary

    I. Lustful parents (a strong sexual appetite is virtually hereditary in certain families).

    II. A sanguine temperament that influences the nervous system: the constitution is weak, delicate.

B. Acquired

    I. Endemic causes. Those that can be ascribed to the climate, geographic latitude, etc. The inhabitants of regions further south are more subject to it than those in the east and west; least prone to it are those in northern areas.[a]

   II. Daily regimen

      1. Corrupted and heat-producing food (this can be attributed to the physical character of wet nurses and the nature of their milk).

      2. Drink not suitable to the age of the child (as in the premature and overuse of coffee, chocolate, and spirits).

      3. Clothes that are too narrow and confining.[b]

      4. Neglect of physical exercise, especially the sedentary life of girls and boys in public schools; or the kind of bodily movement in which the genitals are rubbed, as in certain types of exercise: horseback riding, swinging, tree climbing, etc., etc.

      5. Too much sleep in soft bed coverings, or too little; not sufficiently quiet, especially if two or more children sleep in a single bed.

      6. Daily evacuations that are either too profuse or meager or changed with respect to quality.

  III. Education

      1. Leisure or a lack of things to do—or the reverse, too many—is not suitable to childhood. Lymphatic children are more prone to premature activity, but those who are emotionally sensitive are the least prone. Nothing is more dangerous than to prematurely exercise the faculties of those children who excel in mental ability; and

---

a. The circumcision of the Jews, which is a prophylactic against prematurely developed sexuality, finds its explanation (in this).

b. Frank, *Politia medica*.

most especially to be reviled is that impulse of our age to prematurely cultivate the minds of children in wastefulness and even with harm to the body's natural shape.

2. Children are not accustomed to reining in their libidinal impulses and to subject the motions of their body to reason's control.

In early childhood, there is no difference between walking and other kinds of motion: children who are not satisfied with play, who roll over from one bed to another, who are always restless and from one moment to the next change their position, who constantly pull at their hair or ears, who through swinging about toss themselves or their chair or display some other vice that they call "a habit" require the special attention of their teachers. For such children involuntarily fall into this state, attentiveness falters, their minds become soporific, and all on its own their sexuality wakes up. (I remember an unhappy colleague of mine, Georg C., whom I knew from childhood and who already as a boy, as well as at a more advanced age, presented these symptoms. Always given to this vice, at the age of twenty-five, after hard and drawn-out reflection, he killed himself because he was weary with life.)

3. The premature reading of poetry, stories, or watching comedies that excite the imagination.
4. A premature knowledge of the sex differences between men and women acquired through conversations, books, images, or the very sight itself, if individuals of different sexes take off their clothes with children present.
5. The mystery under which the functions of sexual life are accustomed to be hidden as if with a veil; thus, the curiosity of children is aroused, which is sufficient in itself to bring into existence this vice.

6. An attack on chastity by means of conversations between adults in the presence of children and too much familiarity with persons of the same or the opposite sex.

The accidental cause (which is never, as many postulate, situated in an accumulation of sperm in the semen-bearing tubes) is absolutely this—the cerebral system so excites the imagination that there is involuntary erection and emission of semen. These causes are of the following kinds:

I. Internal

1. Mental causes, already discussed above with structuring causes; these always display an imagination run riot as their source.
2. Various diseased physical states that cause an itching in the genital region and a congestion at the genitals, such as a retention of urine, bladder stones, an enlarged prostate, scabies, or worms (roundworm or pinworm).

II. External

1. Warm, soft bedclothes, an overheated bed, tight-fitting clothes.
2. Rubbing caused by horseback riding, dancing, tree climbing, bouncing on another person's knees, etc.
3. The undressing of the child, as the sight of a nude body to those unaccustomed to it can especially excite the imagination.
4. The most effective and common cause: the direct seduction by nurses,[c] hairdressers, maidservants,[d] classmates,[e] and, to the shame of humanity, also teachers and tutors.

c. There is a nefarious custom among many nurses to put children to sleep by tickling their genitals.

d. I recall a case in which a lustful maidservant tied down the extremities of a twelve-year-old boy with bonds and then stimulated his member until an emission of semen followed.

e. Another case comes to my mind in which a boy shared with his classmates that this was a better method for urinating.

Even with these enumerated, yet many causes remain that nevertheless could easily be included here—but they deserve no particular mention.[2]

On the Opportunities through Which This Vice Is Aroused

The cunning of man in this matter surpasses all belief, and the means for bringing about an emission of semen are manifold; sometimes a simple stimulation by the fingers, sometimes a pin, a bit of wood, a copper ring, a nail, or a stopper answers these longings. Sabatier relates the case of a poor man who by means of the hole in a bathtub practiced masturbation. I am able to recollect another subject who always surrendered to this evil in the presence of women wearing a white belt. His sensitivity became so pathologically elevated that the mere sight of a white belt was enough to excite the flow from his genitals. Everyone—those who are mindful of the many cases that Tissot and his predecessors published—would concede how diverse the imagination's tricks are that cloud the mind of a man. I altogether refrain from relating these so that I do not incur the reproach that has been held against, not undeservedly, many authors who have written about this disease.[3] It is objected that by their overly clear and vivid descriptions they have rather provoked sexual lust than extinguished it.

Although there is no place where that miserable person, corrupted by sexual madness, is not able to submit to this vice—as the insane in hospitals adequately demonstrate by masturbating themselves in the presence of their fellow inmates and, worse yet, in front of spectators—yet there are particular places in which children most especially indulge in this vice. The most common place, and where almost always for the first time the sexual drive is satisfied in a ruinous way, is the bathroom. There, while urinating, either an excited imagination or curiosity easily induces the child to stimulate his penis, which, when repeated, crosses over into masturbation. Also, there is a necessary privacy associated with this place under whose protection the imagination runs free—vividly portraying the suggestive thoughts and, thus, further embellishing these so that the instinct for onanism, so to speak, is aroused. Guilt and religion will be mostly ineffectual in opposing these, and you will not be able to hold the child's attention and protect him from these imaginative fantasies. For others, the absence of their instructors is sufficient for them to busy themselves with sexual desires. Young men of this sort voluntarily nourish the lurking spark through shameless conversation, and the flame of sexuality bursts forth unexpectedly. Even if the conscientious care of the father or teacher prevents many such incursions, night rushes in, which is a time when many things come together for sexual arousal and the cultivation of this disease: most especially privacy, the softness of the bed, the absence of any chaperone, shadows, and sexually titillating dreams. These are increased if there is a long dalliance in bed and after a sumptuous dinner. We see a child succumb to this vice not only in his parent's home but even more often in public and private institutions, in the coming together of a large number of children, especially if two lie together in one bed. In schools themselves, the opportunity for masturbation is not lacking, as students sit at a distance from the teacher—who is most often completely nearsighted—wrapped up in their coats, and by means of their tablets and the students sitting in front of them, they can escape his notice. Finally, there are those places as much for cleaning the body as for working out, places suited to the health of men. I am speaking of the baths, which are found not to be immune from this vice. The unspeakable ways that provide an opportunity for this vice are numerous and great. Therefore, the custodian must take the greatest precaution to guard the child well, to watch over him and gain his full trust. For, otherwise, the diagnosis of this evil as along with its therapy will be more hypothetical than sound.

Description of the Pathology

Erection of the male member follows either from preceding fantasies of the imagination or the direct excitement of the genitals (in part through the swelling of the ischio-cavernosi muscles). The erection, through its own unique nature or by habit, lasts for various amounts of time, until with the spastic contraction of the bulbo-cavernosi muscles the emission of semen occurs. During this act, the man can be said to be almost epileptic: his face swells; the carotid arteries quiver; the eyes involuntarily close; his breathing is more rapid; his pulse is short, fast, and rough; there are convulsive motions in his extremities; the man is not in control of his consciousness but is indifferent, and pays attention to nothing. At that point, the blood is collected in his central organs, and there is often a sudden opportunity for apoplexy[f] or asphyxia or at that time the germs of many diseases can be implanted, which we will study more expansively below. When the last drops of sperm have flowed out of the urethra, the member suddenly relaxes and becomes flaccid, mental functions return, gradually the blood's circulation is subdued, and functions return to normal. The poor soul is repulsed by and detests himself; he regrets that he has sinned, and anxiety over the lost fluids tortures him. Indeed, the weakest

f. Plater presents a case of a man who, advanced in age, was plagued after coitus with attacks of asphyxia, about the danger of which he was not sufficiently warned, so that one time during intercourse he breathed out his soul.

children, who are unable to understand what has happened and are unaware of the consequences, become morosely solitary; they flee from their parents, tutors, and instructors, filled with a firm resolve to abstain from this vice. Yet the recollection alone of the pleasure is enough to arouse the imagination, and a short time later this scene is repeated. For this reason, cultured men and those learned in letters are susceptible to this vice.

It is necessary at this point to briefly touch on an argument that is frequently bandied about. What lays an ambush for the man at a more advanced age—is it repeated intercourse or a form of *Psychopathia sexualis*? There are many who claim[g] that this latter means of satisfying sexual lust is more suitable and less damaging. The man remains free from all those ills that are contracted from an affair with an impure, syphilitic woman and other evils. In order to resolve this question, we must return to one of the first axioms.

Psychopathia sexualis is a disease, while coitus is a state suitable to nature, for this is what "sexual drive" means, and it is hardly difficult to add further arguments:

a. In all the psychopathy there is need for greater stimulation so that the same effect is aroused that in coitus (the dynamic electric joining of differing poles) is produced by the rubbing of the vagina with the male member.
b. Coitus is not able to be repeated so often since—on the flipside—exhaustion forbids it.
c. Often the opportunity for coitus is lacking, whereas incitement to the psychopathy is always available.

g. I would not bring together these arguments, if I had not known in the recent past a thirty-six-year-old man who confided to me that due to various reasons he had never indulged in coitus but, by the sight of naked women, always brought forth a pollution.

d. Many forms of immodesty are absent more from coitus than from masturbation.
e. A sense of regret and a lassitude with life attend only onanism and prevent a healthful state of mind from being regained afterward.
f. Physical love as much as mental is lacking, and man becomes a lower animal.
g. Onanism exercises a harmful effect that is deeply dangerous and is felt throughout the whole organism, whereas moderate intercourse that is suitable to the individual is healthful.

I will speak about these consequences later when I deal with the secondary illnesses that are caused by *Psychopathia sexualis*. At this point, I shall speak briefly only about the bond of the genital system with the other organs and bodily systems of man, so that the reader may more easily understand how so many and such serious diseases of differing natures acknowledge *Psychopathia sexualis* as their first source, and so that a path is laid out for the chapters of my little work concerning those accompanying diseases.

The effects on the human organism are:

A. Idiopathic in the genital system

The genital parts form more swiftly, and puberty appears earlier.[h] The genitals themselves become soft, loose, a premature foreskin does not fully cover the glans (*paraphimosis*), and there is lack of control over erection and emission. Nocturnal pollutions come on during sleep, or without it, which wake the patient in the beginning but then do not disturb his sleep. Pollutions that happen during the day are a complete effusion of sperm [spermatorrhea],

h. Niemayer presents the case of a child who at four years old was addicted to this evil and who by eight already displayed completely developed genitals.

aroused solely by mechanical means such as walking, horseback riding, or evacuation of the bowels—for any irritation or pleasurable sense arouses it. Soon after, it becomes an involuntary penal discharge [gonorrhea], and no erection precedes it; then impotence seizes the adolescent befouled with fatigue (in girls, the menses become irregular and the functioning of the uterus becomes disordered for their entire life).

No one, indeed, will doubt the origin of so many disorders in the sexual sphere that arise from this font. But many believe these depend on the loss of fluid at such crucial moments that is then absorbed by the lymphatic vessels and drawn into the circulatory system. Consequently, coitus ought to display almost the same effect as onanism, but reason and experience reject this with strong arguments. Indeed, I reproach that perverse direction of the sexual faculty that, through constant agitation of such powerful organs weakens the entire genital system, ruins it, and, through the dynamic connection of every organ and system, ought to share in its suffering.

B. Sympathetic

    I. In the brain and nervous system.

The direct anatomical connection of the spermatic plexus through the mesenteric and the splenic with the semilunar plexus and from there via the sympathetic ganglion to the brain and spinal cord is recognized by all, but a few words will suffice to make this clear according to physiology. Impressions coming from the emotions, lustful images, the sight of a nude woman, and, in the frail, merely a certain description (*chronique scandaleuse*) or a conversation with a prostitute all can cause a sudden congestion in the genitals and lead to erections. Mental onanism depends on this affinity. In contrast, the accumulation of a great quantity of semen in the semen-bearing tubes produces an effect[i] on the brain and entire nervous system in a particular way (as with animals the time of Venus's passion). The brain and genital system hold themselves in the following way: as two poles that are engaged in constant action and reciprocal reaction. Thus, in *Psychopathia sexualis*, the imagination breaks the will of a man, even if his rational mind rejects and reviles this deed.

Thus, irritation in one or the other poles causes action, and a consequence of this excited state displays itself in organic life [*vita plastica*] and the animal brain in the form of excessive vitality, hypersthenia, or asthenia (an irritable or listless weakness), and various diseases appear that find their place among the secondary diseases of *Psychopathia sexualis*.

II. In the digestive organs.

According to anatomy, there is a connection through the vagus nerve. There are certain foods that in a unique way increase the sexual drive and do so shortly after eating, including many aromatics, vanilla bean, etc., as well as sharper foods such as some types of pepper, etc.[j] Indeed, the excessive depletion of semen involuntarily urges the patient toward food that is juicy (poached eggs) as if to restore his lost fluids. Driven by this impulse, patients eat more than they digest, and from this they increase the harm or, at least, plant the germs for other kinds of harm. (Broussais

i. I remember a joke of the late most honored Prof. Hermann, who often declared in public that the miracles of the solitary hermits and anchorites could be explained by this.

j. From this, there is the opinion among the public that coitus stimulates the vegetative life, strengthens the organs of digestion, and loosens constipation.

placed it beyond doubt that there is no chronic disease that is not attended by an underlying inflamed state of the stomach or the formation of an ulcer.)[4] I therefore believe that through the great tension in the stomach, especially at this moment when the entire organism is most violently agitated, the stomach's capacity and that of the entire apparatus of reabsorption is increased, and, once the vigor and strength of this system is broken, it more easily succumbs to a harmful external force. By this rationale, it seems to me explained how gastritis, enteritis, and abdominal typhoid kill so many people, how hemorrhoids have become so common, how chlorosis is almost hereditary and arthritis, a disease of the elderly, spares almost no one, and how a thousand such ills of various forms in which the entire digestive system grows sick, now plagues mankind and prematurely ends life's circuit.

III. In the circulatory and respiratory organs

Anatomy demonstrates a direct connection, and physiology confirms it. These parts are certainly in the first instance affected; for, indeed, in the libidinal act, blood is accumulated for a long time in the central organs and from this an excitement of the heart is inflicted and cardiac dilation, aneurysm, and hypertrophy result. In the lungs, the respiratory function is upset and the seed is implanted for a multitude of diseases such as catarrh, blockage of the lungs, emphysema, and tuberculosis.

Diagnosis

Granted that these pernicious effects gradually appear throughout so many systems and organs, and this "wasting disease"—if I may call it that—seeks out both the mental and physical cardinal systems equally and upsets every function of the body, nevertheless, there is no disease whose diagnosis is more difficult and more in doubt than *Psychopathia sexualis*. This is partly because like a serpent it creeps on stealthily and partly because it lacks particularly characteristic symptoms and is easily confused with the onset of other diseases, especially scrofula and worm infestation. In fact, this is an important duty for parents, educators, or those to whom the care of children is entrusted to recognize this disease at its germination and to destroy a sexual drive that has grown excessive. Is not the mental and physical formation of children important to a doctor? And is this psychopathy not a true disease and one that first openly appears in childhood? And then is it not often the case that a parent's helplessness or the inexperience or youth of the teachers is unequal to carrying through this duty, and, therefore, a truly humane doctor and friend to the family ought to speak and carry it out? A final diagnosis is not possible to establish without a complete assessment of the age, sex, and lifestyle of the child, with support from a history of the disease, which is necessary for those who wish to draw the diagnosis from the presenting signs.

The signs that this disease puts forth both in extent and over time are not uniquely suited to *Psychopathia sexualis* and appear in the development of many diseases. For the sake of clarity, however, we separate them into bodily and mental signs, the former into idiopathic and sympathetic.

I. Bodily

1. The idiopathic signs are a hanging and loose scrotum, frequent and involuntary urination and, from this, befouled linens. In girls, a moist vagina with swollen labia and an overly sensitive clitoris.
2. The sympathetic signs are changed color in the face; a great paleness or sudden flush alternating with pallor (however, naturally pale children and frail, irritable children change

their facial color without cause); muscles having become slack (this occurs naturally in phlegmatic children); eyes that are slunk down, bordered with a livid or heavy ring (this occurs by heredity with infestation of intestinal worms);[5] a fixed gaze; lips losing their color (a sign of scrofula); the body's motions are disturbed (either by nature or from some other cause); pimples or small eruptions on the face (nature marks out the sinner); a partial sweat, especially around the genitals or at the tip of the nose; children involuntarily touching their genitals, particularly during sleep;[k] a shaky, staggering gait; fetid breath; a forward-leaning posture; and quivering in the joints.

II. Mental

The child seeks out solitary places, is peevish, easily roused to anger. Children change their character (their mental temperament); various emotional moods are produced, especially fear and terror; a distraction in the mind, scorn for childish games, weeping without reason, and countless other ills make themselves evident, all of which point to an idle mind and sense of reason and also that the imagination is becoming overly strong in a fixed direction.

I have already mentioned that a diagnosis is confirmed through a case history (as in the traces of semen in linens). Parents, teachers, and all those who live with children ought to attentively examine and weigh carefully every opportunity for a sharp judgment—that is, if instructors bewail the sudden incapacity of children in their studies or the constant distractedness of their charges; if different

---

k. Bernt recommends that sleeping children be roused suddenly from sleep. If they are innocent, after having been awoken, they will quietly go back to sleep, but if, in truth, their sexuality was aroused, they move their hands closer to the genitals as almost all those under the sway of onanism sleep with hands placed at their genitals.

methods are brought into use to no avail by either a teacher or others; if, in turn, an ever-increasing weakness makes more credible a suspicion about the advance of this poison. As for the examination of children, this ought to be instituted with the utmost attentiveness, and once a suspicion is afoot, it is better established by a doctor to whom the child is lovingly devoted. The child will more easily confess to the doctor than to his parents or teacher, whose censure, and even punishment, he strongly fears—fear that prevents every confession. A doctor may share with the child the conjecture being made about him, but he will not wait until the child makes a confession, for a child will admit more openly to a doctor making inquiries.

Prognosis

The prognosis in the psychopathy is always grim and restricted by narrow limits, for this is a general disease. Every system and organ either totters under the disease or ever more gradually is afflicted by it. The mind itself, on which healing principally depends, is made intensely ill. [Prognosis] differs according to the following circumstances:

> Age: For the most part, onanism occurs between the seventh and fourteenth year—if prior to that, the disease is more serious and the prognosis more ill-favored; if later, the disease accompanies the man to the day of his death.
>
> [Sex:] The inferior sex contracts fewer harmful effects than the stronger sex; but these crimes of the female sex pass into their offspring.
>
> [Temperament:] The sanguine temperament is most especially troubled, the phlegmatic less so. The melancholic and choleric occur only as a mental type in childhood and at that time are already diseased temperaments.

[Constitution:] A soft, weak constitution under a strong nervous system indeed takes on the worst ills; a solid, straight, or easy constitution, less.

Physique: Unique diseased configurations together with a disease that is lurking and germinating—such as the posture in rickets, scrofula, and physical wasting—accordingly, take on the development of these. Such a physique presents the worst prognosis, for if the afflicted is freed from *Psychopathia sexualis*, the disease coming out from under the wings of it kills the patient.

Advanced diseases: As an afflicted patient was troubled by many diseases, so much the more dangerous are the consequent diseases to be feared.

[Duration:] The length of time during which the illness has lasted. The more recent the illness, the more hope for the diseased to be healed and his health restored through a suitable dietetic regimen and proper therapy.

[Character:] A more acute character to the disease, over time, lays the groundwork for dangers; truly, a chronic nature enervates and drains off every fount of life and prepares the way for death.

Shape of the disease: The more the symptoms appear to be only of damaged sexual function, the better these are noted. However, the more symptoms of the disease that are perceived to be general, as it snakes its way far and wide through every system, the patient is consequently attacked by a more serious disease, and the less hope shines for his health and the more his prognosis hangs in the balance.

Stages: Although in no book do I find mentioned the stages of this type of disease—that is, *Psychopathia sexualis* or onanism as a form of it—nevertheless, so that I may render an easier prognosis and fix more accurately the cases in which we are able to hope for a healthy outcome through therapy, I will attempt to describe these stages.

First stage—sexual life is disturbed and there are symptoms that its function is damaged; the harmonization of the intellectual faculties is elevated; sexuality is predominant.

> Second stage—organic life [*vita plastica*] is disturbed not only
> with respect to the sexual sphere but also in the entire animal
> economy, and the animal life-force shares in the disposition
> (spasms, pains, incomplete paralysis, the first stages of *tabes
> dorsalis*).[6]
> Third stage—all life is failing, whether organic or animal (ad-
> vanced *tabes dorsalis*).

To which of these stages an auspicious outcome corresponds and
to which a contrary, requires no particular explanation.

Therapy

Even when a therapy is selected with the utmost care and adapted
to the specific case, rarely does it correspond to our prayers; even
more rarely does a happy outcome follow upon our efforts. Nevertheless, it is only right that a doctor at least try this therapy and,
according to medical laws and general principles, cure the disease.

It will take but a few words to sketch out at this point the pre-
cepts of such a cure. Every therapy ought to depend on some rationale particular to the essential nature of the disease that the
doctor wishes to heal. I apply this thesis, already circulated by the
ancients, to this disease. Masturbation as a particular type of *Psychopathia sexualis* consists in an overly powerful sexuality. Every
mental function is drowned in this instinct; memory constantly
recalls general stimulations that arouse this sexuality. The imagination confuses all the impressions that take in with our external
senses and continuously places pleasure before the eyes. The mind
recognizes that this vice is truly abominable, but, abandoned by
all its strength, the heightened imagination is master over it, and,
lulled by a deep lethargy, little by little it grows dull: the will no
longer readily obeys reason but, rather, acknowledges the sexual

instinct as its master. The man drawn on, as I say, by a sexual madness not only does not avoid any opportunity for arousing this instinct, but he even seeks it out. If he succumbs, then he makes excuses by persuading himself that the opportunity proved too strong, and he resolves to flee from other such occasions when he might repeat whichever is his vice. But the poor man, led on by this foul madness, lets go of his free will and involuntarily is compelled to an even more outrageous deed. This psychopathy is involved in a causal connection with the genital system in which the primitive irritating effect is priapism, which manifests in the emission of semen under increasingly the most trivial of stimuli, then in pollutions occurring night and day and in the repressed support of this system. This system, once irritated, offers an opportunity for repetitions of its particular inclinations, and thus it brings on the spread of the disease's effects into every system and organ. We can perceive this clearly if we consider that in an organ wracked with disease that there is an inclination to many diseases. What surprise is it if a weakened genital system and one in a state of oversensitive infirmity more easily surrenders to this evil than a healthy system enjoying its natural strength? From this, it is evident that in such diseased individuals trivial stimulations suffice to provoke its normal course and augment its irritable state of weakness. The primary effects clearly are propagated through the connection of the nerves to the sympathetic system, spinal cord, and brain. The heart and circulatory system become allies to this evil, and in its final attack, the entire vegetative system—digestion, the reabsorption (of nutrients), their circulation and nutrition itself—is not able to be found unimpaired.

I omit the ruinations and derangements that this disease causes in individual organs and systems. The pathologic anatomy spreads into almost every organ, showing tuberculosis, typhoidal crasis, the softening of tissue, tumors, etc. Clearly, these organic changes have their rich source in the present evil.

With this preface, a rational therapy, if we are to hope anything from it, relies on the following general principles seeing that each particular doctor must modify it for the individual, making selections according to the afflicted system and the level of affliction. This disease, in which the psyche and physical nature grow ill, requires a doubled method of cure, psychological (dynamic) and physical (material).

Method for Psychological Cure

In order that the intellectual faculties be released from this contagion (if you pardon the expression), we ought to use every aid available to us. In truth, the distraction of the mind and its occupation stand out among the psychological remedies. For the internal senses as much as the external should be occupied by diverse means so that their attention is drawn away from sexuality, the heightened imagination is suppressed, the domination of sexuality is broken, and the will is yoked under the mastery of reason. I believe that music especially merits a doctor's attention, as it exerts the most healthful power over the senses—but not that style of song that is called "romance" by the French, and not southern musical drama, but instead especially the serious music of the Germans and ecclesiastic chant. For the cleansing of the imagination and mind and extinguishing sexuality's spark, the study of the sciences, which are tested by experience, may not be without purpose[1]—that is, natural and universal history, chemistry, and

1. Oken, *Naturgeschichte für alle Stände*. Virey, *Histoire naturelle du genre humain*.

physics, in fact even a certain knowledge of the human body's anatomy and its physiology. It will be of the utmost importance to convince adult men, youths, and even children concerning the unspeakable nature of this vice that they commit, and by this persuasion be able to instruct the afflicted with a triple curriculum: religious, moral, and physiological. For the mind must first understand the shamefulness and danger of this deed, and then be filled with a firm resolve, both for not seeking out a moment to begin, as well as fleeing far from it altogether. With all these combined, we certainly can hope for something of health with regard to the psychological faculties. Let us now move along at this point to the physical method of effecting a cure.

Method for Physical Cure

This treatment is entirely general, and it will be for the doctor to modify this for each individual case. At the outset, these essential points seem best:

1. All inciting influences provoking an attack of the disease are diligently to be avoided, the diseased tendency for this evil corrected, and the diseases that nourish this psychopathy remedied. This requirement is fulfilled by a complete understanding of the etiological causes, which we already set forth more expansively, and through the greatest level of care that a doctor ought to direct at this disease. The psychological and physical treatment responds to his entreaties and is as much a lifestyle regimen as a preventative one, and even the therapy itself is called on to offer support.
2. The harmful effects in the human body that appear in different organs and systems according to their nature, force, and form are to be destroyed or, at any rate, lessened.
3. A recurrence is to be prevented with the utmost care, for in this disease recurrence is more dangerous, secondary diseases are more complicated, and a recovery more difficult.

With these therapeutic indications a cure that is as much psychological as physical is sufficient, and especially one under both a lifestyle approach and therapy.

Thus, physical treatment divides into one that is related to lifestyle and one that is therapeutic.

On Lifestyle[7] Treatment

This must be general in nature and ought to take into consideration the following:

1. The diet should be simple, easy on the digestion, and not savory with aromatics. In the strictest sense it should be a homeopathic diet, neither producing too much stomach acid nor conducive to creating too much chyme. Foodstuffs should be selected more from the vegetable kingdom than the animal. From the latter, only fresh milk, whey, veal, and chicken are allowed. Forbidden are hard-boiled eggs, brined meat, that which is smoke-dried, the meat of game, oysters, and crabs, etc., butter and cheese. From the vegetable kingdom most preferable are fresh vegetables such as spinach, cabbage, watercress, wild carrot—less the potato. Among pulses the simple are to be selected, and those should be in a meager quantity neither rich with aromatics nor with too much sugar or fermented. Food should be stretched out over a number of repeated meals in small doses. Beware of dinner.[8] During the evening hours, a broth made with bread suffices for children, and for adults, vegetable lemonade or squeezed vegetable juice.
2. Drink should be simple; most suitable is pure chilled water. Spirited drink is to be avoided, especially the Arabian drink and tea (Chinese or Russian); only beverages prepared from the acorn or Icelandic moss should be offered to those who are weaker.
3. Clothes should not be too tight and constricting, and trousers should not be too large; beware of belts. Linen [underthings]

deserve special care, since they confirm a diagnosis and give away the diseased in the further course of the illness.[m]

4. The air is to be pure, chilled by frequent ventilation.
5. Bodily movement should be suitable to the nature of the patient, the stage of the disease, and the level of infirmity. Motion should be active. Chiefly to be recommended is a morning walk or one before lunch in a garden, field, or forest. And, if strength permits, an excursion into the mountains so that the beauty of the region may delight the soul and restore it to its natural state.

It is the teacher's duty to transfix the attention of the child and by doing this explain to him the phenomena of nature. He should attempt to stir in the boy a love of collecting plants or insects or butterflies; but the teacher should always watch the child and not abandon him for a minute. Thus, going for a walk strikes a double target: it will increase the body's strength and purge the imagination. At the beginning, the time devoted to the walk should be brief and then gradually extended for a longer period. The place for the walk should be changed so that the same sight repeated for the hundredth time will not bore the children. A walk is recreation, not, in truth, a punishment.

There are, moreover, certain signs of sickness that either prohibit a walk or restrict it within more confined limits. These signs warn the child's caretaker in particular that he ought to speak about the child's state with a doctor and ask his opinion concerning the type of walk that is appropriate. These signs are:

A headache, an easily changeable color to the face, rapid or troubled breathing, heart palpitations, easily breaking into a sweat especially in the armpits, easily becoming tired, etc. It is difficult to distinguish the exhaustion arising from the exertion of bodily strength from the weakness that owes its origin to an error in that very bodily strength. Yet, certainly, other

---

m. I knew a patient who always tied up his limbs with dirty underlinens and, thus, excited a flow into his genitals; he then placed his erect penis between his limbs and from this conjured forth an emission of sperm.

symptoms occur that a doctor can correctly evaluate. Hunting can be allowed only when the disease is broken and the body has regained its strength. At that time, even greater oversight is required so that solitude does not cause the disease to recur. For this reason, hunting ought to be considered among the doubtful lifestyle remedies.

The art of gymnastics offers various ways for the doctor to increase the body's strength through prescribing the practice of fixed movements. In gymnastics, usually only one part of the body or layer of muscle is engaged by the exercises, while the others remain at rest. In *Psychopathia sexualis* an equal movement of all the muscles is required, so that all vital functions are aroused by this harmonization, while nutrition and restoration of the entire body is animated. In turn, a certain level of vigor is demanded for such gymnastic exercises, which is certainly lacking in patients laboring under this disease, and the exhaustion that we are able to observe already in the first attack will prohibit all further gymnastic exercises.

Of all the types of the gymnastic art, I prefer swimming during the summertime. It provides for cleanliness of the body, and by its active movement strains all the muscles equally, and, on account of the medium with which the body comes in contact, it supplies the greatest advantage to the patient.[9] Everything else related to *Psychopathia sexualis* has to do with etiology rather than therapy.

I judge every movement that causes sensitivity to be more harmful than useful. To be conveyed in a carriage can be allowed only to the frail and when no hope shines for restoring the patient's health, so that we may alleviate just for a moment the patient's misfortune and hold out to him the hope of recovering his health, which makes his passing less terrible. The psychopathy has this particular aspect—namely, that a patient who is aware of his condition believes that he is ruined in an irretrievable way and places no faith in the entire field of medicine. He does not seek out a doctor and even recoils from his help. He begs relief from a priest and seeks religious consolations, believing that God alone can save him, and, thus, he renders every therapy all the more difficult.

Less advisable is horseback riding, which I have already included among the originary causes. The body's movement then deserves a place among the lifestyle remedies if it is practiced safely and adapted to each case. For that reason it is up to a doctor to prescribe the exercise. One who has carefully weighed these prescriptions may be able to offer more of an advantage than one who supposes that he can cure every disease, which most often is the case with junior doctors.

6. Sleep should be brief and only at night. A child may seek its bed at the eighth or ninth hour, and eight or nine hours are suitable for rest. The bed should have firm bedclothes, the sheets should be of simple linen and not overly warm. The child should often rise from bed during the night, and the one who is supervising him should draw near to the sleeping child and observe him. He will be able to recognize from the changed physiognomy if the boy is seized by a pleasurable dream. If this is the case, the child must be awoken immediately, and it is even better if he abandons his bed for a short time. In a patient already afflicted with diseased pollutions, the immediate cleansing of the genitals through the application of cold water can be called into use.

It is especially important that the boy keeps his hands above the covers. This should be demanded of him most severely, and if a diseased habit is already in control so that he involuntarily plunges his hands below the covers, then there is need for the greatest watchfulness. From the moment the caretaker realizes what is happening, he ought to immediately order the boy to wake up and be deprived of sleep. In a repeated case, a strong punishment should be inflicted, and it is better that the boy stay awake all night than sleep in that fashion. Many mechanisms are recommended that are said to hinder the patient, so that he puts his hands less frequently close to his genitals. Yet such an apparatus, which not only prevents this but also impedes all friction of the male member, is still sought from the field of medical bandaging.[10] Every bond and shackle that is applied to the hands, because it hinders the reflexes and brings about swelling, actually advances the evil. For this reason, inexperienced teachers, who are not equal to this matter, contribute to the disease's further progression.[11] Here, with the kind indulgence of my reader, I will add a few words concerning children's bed-wetting. A mother complains that her child labors under bed-wetting, and for this reason the child is punished. But the disease to which bed-wetting as a symptom owes its origin is overlooked, and the parents treat the "bed-wetting" although they do not perceive the disease lurking underneath. But, truly, bed-wetting, as I have very often had the occasion of observing, is nothing other than a symptom of *Psychopathia sexualis*; it requires no special treatment and vanishes on its own once the disease is removed. I admit it is a difficult task to watch over a child by day and night with such great attention, but I believe that it offers junior doctors an opportunity to excel and to save the entire race for humankind, and citizens for the state. I would believe it to be of no little use, if children, afflicted with this evil, were handed over, at least for a time, to the care of doctors.[n] I certainly anticipate more health from such a method than by a therapy chosen with the greatest precision but lacking the watchfulness and vigilance that is demanded of teachers but is rarely found in them. The wealthy of every region deserve special censure, in my opinion, for this reason—led on by a too intense and unthinking zeal for the Gallic language, they hand their children over to French caretakers, without knowing whether they have the faculties of soul and character that a children's teacher should have. Parents beg a cure for *Psychopathia sexualis* from a doctor, yet they abandon their child to the custody of these sorts of people, under whose auspices the disease perfected itself.

n. By no means, however, [should they be handed over] to medical students. At Vienna the most wretched practice is that teachers are selected from those who either love their studies and then disregard the child or else neglect their studies, and then certainly the child draws little use from such negligent men.

It seems to me that a teacher is not always immune from fault if *Psychopathia sexualis* develops in a child who is entrusted by the parents to his protection and guardianship. Truly, it is the duty of this caretaker to guard against the evil, to suppress dormant sexuality, and, if a seed of disease becomes evident, to immediately make the parents more aware of the condition of the child and the necessity of a cure.

But there are parents and tutors who—I do not know whether from ignorance or a frivolity of spirit—slight this and only seek the help of a doctor once the disease has developed to a higher stage, and the doctor is then able to offer nothing but to be an ineffective observer of the organs' ruination. I say this repeatedly, and I will say it more often: at the beginning of the disease much is able to be done; if, however, the disease has advanced to the point where every system feels the wound, many things are tried, but little is to be hoped for.

7. Cleanliness of the body: washing not only the face but the whole body, to which the child can become gradually accustomed, especially washing the nape of the neck and the genitals; and a cold sitz bath before sleep.[12] Washing of the genitals with cold water during the night justly occupies the first place somewhere between a lifestyle remedy and a therapeutic one.

8. Finally, regarding secretions and excretions, the damaged functioning of these requires medical treatment. But in the case of lighter disturbances, a lifestyle change is suitable. Let the bowels be free and have a movement every day. If they are slow, as in scrofulous children, a purging anti-inflammatory answers every entreaty: sugared cold water in the morning, milk-sugar, whey, prune pulp, manna,[13] a mild infusion of senna, and rhubarb—beware of the stronger purgative salts. Diarrhea in sensitive patients arising from an irritation of the intestines through the connection of the spermatic and the splanchnic nerves requires no particular therapy: chocolate, bread sop, cacao, salep,[14] grana sago,[15] etc., or a small dose of rhubarb or ipecac (beware of opium) will repay all of our efforts. Skin that is soaking wet, especially in the armpits, deserves the attention

of the teacher. Too much active motion and too much exertion of the intellectual faculty are to be avoided. Food should be of the vegetable kind. In such sweats, a cold bath is most salutary. Bleeding from hemorrhoids ought to be addressed by a doctor with greater caution, as it warns of a danger to the afflicted areas. Each [symptom] demands its own cure according to general laws and particular therapy. Urine is worthy of a doctor's attention; often semen swims in it like a wisp of wool, gradually floats to the bottom and can be distinguished by a unique odor. Patients blame this for causing a slump in the strength of their urine's flow, which to the patient seems exceedingly increased. This increase in quantity is not absolute but only relative and is joined with a lower level of incontinence, which is sufficiently explained by the irritated bladder (from the continuity of the mucosal membrane) and the prostate. A suppressed psychopathy will cause even this symptom to dissipate; but if it more strongly troubles the patient, then leeches and narcotic ointment applied to the anus will be of some aid.

I now enter into the most precarious place of my work, for there is a massive farrago of remedies as many from the mineral kingdom as from the vegetable and animal that are vaunted by so many and such great doctors with the highest of praise. In this itself, it seems to me, lies the principal cause for the decline of medical practice in our age and the lesser faith in medical science. Because doctors only increase the pharmacological thesaurus with new appendices, they are less intent to examine and confirm the experience of older doctors at the bedside of patients. Doctors object to me that they are forced to revert to these new remedies and try them alone since older drugs do not respond entirely to every wish of the doctor. But I ask, what is the benefit of listing in the pharmacopoeia a remedy that lacks a healthful effect? Would it not be better to reduce the pharmacological collection and to call a remedy only those materials whose effect is confirmed from antiquity and whose healthful action is daily manifest at the patient's bedside? Is it not dangerous for a junior doctor, who lacks guidance in diagnosis of diseases, to be uncertain and doubtful when he is selecting the weapons for subduing the enemy? Every salesman praises his wares, and so does every doctor his remedies, which he uses out of habit and believes are his unique secrets—but the survival instinct overcomes the opinions of the specifist[16] and saves the man.

With these preliminaries, I proclaim the thesis that onanism is especially difficult to cure (as is easily understood, every *Psychopathia sexualis* is an example of a class) against which so many specific remedies are recommended by today's most eminent doctors and those of previous generations. Let me remain silent regarding the authors who have given their life's work to this matter, for the physicians who have handled this subject are rarer than the educators who have contributed much to investigating its origin and confirming its diagnosis. But in terms of treatment, they have done little. Filled with a sincere desire to avoid the mistake that is committed in so many pharmacologies and being convinced that one true remedy[o] is effective with a strength more powerful than a hundred remedies about whose effects we are uncertain—some of these uncertain remedies being praised by one, and rejected by another—at this point I will present the opinions only of some authorities and will abstain from an excessively broad list of the opinions of diverse pathologists.

Haase[p] strongly recommends camphor, as much to be applied internally in the form of an emulsion or powder as externally

o. Whose benign action in the human body falls every day into observation and comes ever more into use.

p. *Über die Erkenntniss und Cur der chronischen Krankheiten von Dr. Wilhelm Andreas Haase*, vol. 3, part 1, sec. 130, p. 134.

rubbed in the pubic region on the perineum and dorsal spine.[17]
The most illustrious Neumann rejects camphor absolutely for
this kind of illness; he goes so far as to declare it injurious.[q] My
few experiments, when I applied this in the form of a poultice to
the genitals in repeated succession, never proved to me the old
adage: "Camphor with its odor castrates men through the nose."
And I do not expect anything from a remedy whose physical character, because it is prepared from tree sap by means of distilla-
tion, and chemical properties[r] assign it to a place among resinous
remedies such that attack the urogenital system with a particular force. These promote both its secretions and excretions (the
excitatory force of phlogistic diuretics is proven without a doubt
on the fevered nerves of older patients and on contagious typhus
for younger ones) and, to the present day, its scent even for those
dying in great hospitals is offered as a restorative before their
death. I altogether reject the truth of the proverb just now related;
perhaps for past authorities there was something of a joke in this
saying, and posterity believed in it as being tried and tested and
did not dare to overthrow a maxim so often recited. I never hope
for much in the human organism from the delivery of a remedy
through the nose—except for sneezing powders—and I believe
that camphor applied in this manner has the same outcome as so
many homeopathic remedies that are boasted to equally relieve
diarrhea and take away catarrh.[s] But the fact that camphor enjoys
a healthful effect in so many afflictions of the urogenital system

q. *Von den Krankheiten des Menschen: Spec. Pathologie und Therapie von
Dr. Carl Georg Neumann,* vol. 1, p. 782.

r. Insoluble in water, soluble in vinous spirits; carbogenic and hydrogenic
elements.

s. What is the surprise? An exalted fantasy paves the way for so many illnesses,
why should it not be able to relieve them?

(as in difficulty urinating, diseased pollutions, priapism, and satyriasis) does not in any way contradict my opinion. For, certainly,
an opposite vital character produces the same diseased symptoms.
I in no way deny the benign action of this drug in all those illnesses
for which there is another vital character, in particular when an
exhaustive or numbing weakness is latent. However, that it alone
is effective for the kind of symptoms that relate to an aggravated
weakness—such as those that follow *Psychopathia sexualis*—that
I emphatically deny. Hartmann[t] confirms my opinion in saying:
Camphor is especially recommended in that type of difficult or
painful urination that the pungency of Spanish Fly has introduced, in diseased pollutions, in priapism, satyriasis, melancholy,
and mania arising from masturbation. In difficult or painful urination he provides the cause to which its origin is owed, and in
the others, since he talks about the deviation of mental function, it
shall be right for me to suppose that the sluggishness of the genital
system is an exhausted weakness. Sobernheim[u] expresses almost
the exact same idea, saying: The power to suppress irritated genitals is attributed to camphor, and for this reason it is considered
a moderating agent, but it only has this power under a particular
condition and method, and in contrast it presents the opposite
and invigorating effect in the normal state. (Scudery saw that erections, pollutions, and sexual fantasy in sleep followed after its application.)[18] Every simple man today can recognize the symptoms
of disease, but to distinguish the immediate cause of each affliction from the underlying one and fight it with fitting remedies
is the duty of a doctor. Haase considers even narcotics worthy of

t. *Pharmacologia dynamica* Caroli Hartmann, vol. 2, p. 102.
u. Dr. Joseph Friedrich Sobernheim, *Handbuch der praktischen Arzneimittel-
lehre*, 1 Lieferung, 160.

mention, especially opium, henbane, and belladonna. But, indeed, I ask, what should be expected from narcotics in an illness in which the emotive life lies idle through its own power and the vegetative system requires arousal rather than depression? Opium, moreover, certainly at the outset excites the circulatory system, and every incitement of the blood vessels ought to be strenuously avoided in *Psychopathia sexualis*. In addition, opium is most rarely used in treating small children on account of its power to restrain the bowels. The most illustrious reformer of medicine, Schoenlein,[v] has rejected all specificist therapy and judges the precipitating causes to be worthy of greater attention. He returns every method of a cure rather along the lines I have first indicated. Among the remedies for quieting genital irritation he recommends external remedies such as washing the perineum with cold water with salt, ammonia, and vinegar added. For internal use, he recommends camphor with nitrate and opium, according to this formula:

R   one grain of potassium nitrate
two grains of camphor
half a grain of pure opium
one scruple[19] of white sugar
M. D. S.[20] Before going to sleep

He also praises baths prepared from a cold infusion of wild marrow, and injections of this remedy into the urethra and vagina,[w] as well as cold poultices placed at the nape of the neck. In his *Pathologia speciali* I find little concerning *Psychopathia sexualis*, and everything explained there[x] refers more to the treatment of

v. Schoenlein, *Specielle Pathologie und Therapie*, 94.
w. In many cases of a white exudate, I have applied this remedy with most felicitous success.
x. Atrophy of the spinal cord.

tabes dorsalis,[21] in which this therapy surely responds to all our hopes, if a hope glimmers that the man is able to be saved in whom this most horrible disease has taken a foothold. Therefore, I abstain from every opinion related to the cure of this disease, having judged it superfluous, since Schoenlein, with the greatest clarity, has sufficiently indicated the way that we ought to follow to weaken this disease.

The most illustrious Neumann[y] offers few words concerning *Psychopathia sexualis*. He always advises that a prostate exam be administered through the anus, and if the prostate has swelled or is found to have increased in volume then he urges mechanical pressure as the most appropriate course of action. In practice he recommends a binding like that for a hernia that should at least compress the perineum.[z] He attributes much to these mechanical pressures for alleviating daily pollutions, particularly those that are accompanied by evacuation of the bowels. Moreover, he orders the patient to be bathed twice daily—the lower spine, buttocks, genitals, and loins—with a chilled vinous spirit or wine made

y. *Von den Krankheiten des Menschen, von Dr. Carl Georg Neumann*, Spec. Pathologie und Therapie, vol. 1, p. 782.

z. Er bedient sich einer Feder, wie zum Bruchband, mit einer kegelförmigen Pelotte; sie wird mittelst einer TBinde so angelegt, dass die Pelotte gerade aufs Perinaeum dringt und längs der Gesässfalte festliegt; das Bauchstück der TBinde besteht aus 2 ledernen Riemen, einen höher als den anderen, die die Feder in ihrer Lage erhalten. Die Pelotte wird an den untersten Riemen noch durch 3 schmale Bänder aus doppeltem Barchet befestigt, die an der Gefässfalte der anderen Seite und zu beiden Seiten des Scrotums nach vorne durchgehen. [He uses a spring, such as a truss, together with a conical pad. It is designed in such a way in the shape of a T-sling that the pad reaches just to the perineum and lies along the buttocks. The bottom of the sling consists of two leather straps, one higher than the other, which hold the spring in position. The pad is fastened to the lower strap with three narrow bands of doubled Barchet that pass through the crease of the buttocks to the other side and around both sides of the scrotum.]

from grain or vinegar or that he be washed with a mixture of these remedies. Internally, he claims quinine as a panacea and prescribes the following formula:

R   One ounce of pulverized Peruvian bark[22] (best quality)
      Half a dram of nutmeg
      Two drams of golden orange-peel
      As much orange-peel syrup as needed
      so that it becomes a soft lozenge[23]

He orders that the dose be ever gradually increased.

Camphor, Neumann says, and similar specifics have no effect against pollutions and only increase fever. As for perineal binding, I have had no opportunity for observing its effect on a sick patient, and for that reason I advise that it be applied only if the prostate is swollen[aa] or its volume is increased (as the author himself concedes), and then it is indicated only when the genitals have no irritation. Since I cannot imagine the genitals in the first stage without any irritation, the remedy—since it excites pressure in the vicinity of the genitals—seems to me full of risk. Indeed, the danger would seem to be increased, if we recognize how difficult it is to make it so that such a binding adheres firmly in a location when every solid pad fails as a base. Every movement, either because it is not immediately felt by the patient or is not tolerated by a lustful boy, on account of the pressure in the scrotum, is most injurious. The application of this binding should be circumscribed within the most narrow limits and is only appropriate in cases in which there is an underlying organic mutation. I am persuaded that there

---

aa. It is rather more possible to refer this to the diseases following upon the *Psychopathia sexualis*.

is a healthful effect from cinchona in all illnesses with an advancing languor of the vital functions, especially as I have often administered an aromatic tincture[bb] of cinchona bark with happy success in afflicted adults laboring under *Psychopathia sexualis*. But in the treatment of children, I find this remedy less convincing, for in children there are many factors that come together that contraindicate cinchona:[cc]

a. The greater weakness of the entire body combined with an intolerance for stimuli. And, indeed, where does this come to our attention more than in effeminate children who are habituated to onanism?
b. Slowness of digestion and assimilation. In the beginning stages of *Psychopathia sexualis* neither of these are slowed down, and the stomach behaves as if it has a general irritation. Because of this, the child eats more than he digests, and gastric deposits are generated that prohibit the use of cinchona. On account of its astringent force, cinchona restricts secretions and excretions, and through this action it closes the bowels. But in sick children a free digestive system is certainly desirable, especially for those affected by this disease, where a closed bowel moves the congestion to the noble organs and threatens them with danger. In the later progression of the disease, the slowness of digestion and assimilation that increases daily restricts the use of cinchona bark to within narrow limits.
c. The lymphatic vessels are as yet inert and less passable; the glands and abdominal viscera are swollen, impacted, and obstructed. Yet scrofulous *dyscrasia*[24] so pervasively slithers through the human race that it is certainly possible to claim that a great number of

bb. This formula:
℞ Half an ounce of tincture of aromatic cinchona bark (Ph. Austrian)
Two drachms of Hallerius's acidic elixir
Emptied into a glass. Let the patient take 15–30 drops in the evening.
cc. Ph. Carl Hartmann, *Pharmacologica dynamica*.

our patients are affected by this failing. In the remaining children who are immune to scrofula, there is often an association of this disease with the second stage of *Psychopathia sexualis*. For life's organic perception senses a change in the humors, and through the more intense functioning of the assimilative faculties wants to restore the loss.[25] An indirect weakness,[dd] however, follows on every excessive exertion of some system, and it is much easier, if by stimulation (that is, exertion of the sexual system) for an irritative weakness of the sensitive and motor faculty to increase day by day. Thus, in children born with scrofula, as much as in those where scrofula follows on *Psychopathia sexualis*, it should be applied more infrequently. Neumann himself, in the part where he discusses scrofula, says: Cinchona bark in scrofula, in which there is an underlying weakness of assimilation, is without utility. Doctors extol this remedy with high praises, but in scrofula it has no power. Only if the children's strength has slipped greatly by use of laxatives and of quicksilver, and if the doctors then cease this method the patients will get better, but not from using cinchona bark but rather from stopping the use of mercury.

As I have had the occasion to observe, cinchona mixed with a certain acid is better suited to adults who still have sensation, and especially in those cases where the vegetative life is less compromised. That is, those cases in which the noxious effect of the psychopathy has restricted itself more to the genital sphere, and daily pollutions come forth in which the nutrition of the genitals is compromised and there is a true exhaustion of this system: ejaculation is very easily excited, and there is no extended or only a very brief erection. (Such spermatorrhea owes its origin not only to *Psychopathia sexualis* but also to the abuse of intercourse—an aberrant sexual drive in the most broad definition.) I can recommend

dd. Hartmann, *Pathologia generalis*.

the following from my experience to patients so afflicted: a cold-prepared infusion of cinchona bark, a tincture of cinchona, or the invigorating elixir of Whyttius in combination with the acidic elixir of Hallerius, cold baths, hip baths, genital bathings with cold water, douches and cold poultices on the base of the neck and on the genitals, and, at the same time, the use of a simple suspension device constructed from silk cloth as indicated that assiduously prevents all friction of the genitals—all of these offer the best results.

I ask pardon for having digressed with these few words concerning an illness altogether different, being about the excessively repeated act of coition; but it concerns itself with similar matters, and this disease has so much affinity with *Psychopathia sexualis* that one can transform into the other. Certainly this quantitative abuse of the sexual faculty germinates as a qualitative aberration during childhood and then grows with young adulthood and returns no benefits to the man.

As for iron—it is never indicated for use in *Psychopathia sexualis*. For a remedy that promotes the manufacture of blood and makes the blood more plastic is certainly contraindicated for a disease that has a concomitant irritation of the veins. It is only a drug remedy for the consecutive diseases of *Psychopathia sexualis* and, above all, for those injuries that manifest as disturbances of the motor faculties or some other parts of sensation. I have seen many patients who were healed by use of the ferruginous waters,[ee] those of Eger and Marienbad and the mud of Pösthen, and I have had the opportunity to observe the power of these waters in such patients. I remember a man of thirty-four years who, after the lightest

ee. Osann, *Darstellung der Heilquellen von Europa.*

labor, felt that his hands were fatigued (it was from writing), so that gradually, he was not able to write to any great extent. The man, otherwise completely healthy, was not aware of any cause for this illness, but from repeated conversations it seemed to me that *Psychopathia sexualis* was the cause of his malady. The internal use of water that is called Franzensquelle, together with baths under the auspices of the now deceased eminent Dr. Conrath, restored to him complete motor function, and, as he confessed to me afterward in Vienna, the malady never returned.[26]

The celebrated reputation of the waters at Marienbad, Eger, Carlsbad, and Pösthen as antispastic and antiparalytic remedies is owed in no small amount to their benign effect on the secondary diseases of *Psychopathia sexualis*. Even so, I put greater faith in cold waters than in warm because, in general, heat is not suitable for a situation in which the genital system suffers from a weakness, whether irritated or torpid; and thereafter, I uncovered for myself why some patients—even if not a great many—are compelled to leave the warm waters of the Carolinen spring to seek out cold waters. My collected experiments allow me to conclude that all ferruginous waters (but especially those more potent in iron) are more suited as baths than used internally, and always in combination with alkaline waters rather than acidulous ones (Marienbad, Kreuzbrunn) because otherwise a spark of underlying irritation could suddenly burst forth and render the cure completely useless, even harmful.[27] Health can be regained even for an entrenched paralysis from the use of iron-heavy mud, but more in the form of a local bath than a general one. The most illustrious Schoenlein recommends a bathing douche with ferruginous waters from Brückenau, Bocklet, Pyrmont, Wiesbaden, etc. I myself witnessed as best an effect from a douche at Pösthen as from one using cold water, particularly in frigid waters flowing from this source. Copper baths (with free carbonic acid) excite the blood's movement to the genitals and increase the heat there, a fact that anyone who uses this bath can perceive. Hence, their application should be limited and perhaps ought to be extended only in desperate cases of virile impotence.

I could have adduced many other remedies, and it would not have been a difficult task to read through several pathologies and using these to describe the medications recommended by the authors. But what good is it for my book or for this disease, which I want to combat, when I have not been able to offer anything except the opinions of various authors whose opinions lack, in my opinion, any practical experience. Since an increased number of weapons can only make the selection more difficult. To which I may add my fear that a young man, ignorant of medical knowledge, reading through my little work can conclude from the treasury of amassed remedies that the healing of this disease is rather easy, but, thus, because of his imprudence, he would err and indeed err quite strongly.

I shall remain silent, therefore, concerning other authorities, and although I have made the investigation and cure of this psychopathy my life's goal, I shall wait for a later time to subject the opinions of diverse pathologists to a strict examination and to transmit the summation of my own studies to public judgment.

From these rather broad expositions, the following theses stand out:

1. Camphor is suitable only for aberrations arising from a numbing weakness of the sexual system.
2. Opium is always more harmful than helpful in *Psychopathia sexualis*.
3. Neumann's perineal binding ought to be applied only for pollutions that owe their origin to a mutation of the prostate.

4. Cinchona bark is suited more for spermatorrhea from the abuse of coitus and for *Psychopathia sexualis* in the second or third stage, and is more suited for adults than children.
5. Cold water holds the preeminent place in every therapy for *Psychopathia sexualis*, even in the work of Neumann and Schoenlein.
6. In the case of diseases developing out of *Psychopathia sexualis*, cold ferruginous waters are indicated more than warm.
7. The external use of ferruginous water is more to my liking than used internally, but it ought always to be combined with solvent water (as from Kreuzbrunn).
8. Ferruginous waters are especially to be applied in cases of partial paralysis.
9. For total paralysis, ferruginous mud in the form of localized baths is suitable.
10. A shower with ice-cold ferruginous waters is especially suitable.
11. In virile impotence, an air-bath may perhaps prove useful.
12. The patient who wishes to make use of healthful waters should be sure to direct his physician to write out a history of his disease, and the physician should not fail to transcribe this account correctly and assiduously.

In the foregoing section, I reviewed the opinion of the most illustrious men with a critical eye and have pointed out in a rather strict manner the cases in which the medications of these men deserve application. But now I will dare to develop a methodology and way that I wish to follow in curing *Psychopathia sexualis*.

The therapy for this disease, as for any other, divides into the preventative, the radical, and the palliative.[28]

Prophylactic therapy requires a psychical and lifestyle treatment, as I have set out previously, and ought to be adapted to each individual case.

Although, in the preceding sections, I have reported everything more expansively that refers to this, I purposely omitted one cause [of the psychopathy],[ff] about which I must say a few words—most obviously concerning the life of the sexual system (*das Geschlechtsleben, die Geschlechtlichkeit*) that varies considerably according to the different stages of the life cycle. In earliest childhood, parents and guardians should be cautious when they select those to whom they entrust their children—namely, nurses, governesses, tutors, and teachers. The practice of handing children over for a long time to the care of tutors is full of danger. Servants who attend younger children in school or in other places of instruction or put on their clothes, especially those who play with the children,[gg] all require the highest order of vigilance from the parents, and their moral character ought to be most stringently examined lest sexuality's fire (*der Geschlechtlichkeit*) be stoked prematurely or—what is accustomed to happen more frequently—the disease itself is imparted by these attendants. The inclinations of children in institutions and schools ought to be scrutinized. The professor should be a physiognomist, as it is already possible to draw conclusions from a disturbed physiognomy. But, if a suspicion arises, then he should immediately separate the child from the others and subject him to special care and tutelage. As for adolescence, precautions should be taken so that youthful lust is not aroused prematurely. Hence, I think that,

---

ff. For sexuality (*Geschlechtlichkeit*) pertains neither to the lifestyle nor to the psychical part of therapy, but, nevertheless, it should be especially taken into consideration in the presentation of *Psychopathia sexualis*.

gg. A case is known to me of a boy who most particularly loved the friendship of girls and who always enjoyed tying together the girls' hands. Later, at the age of puberty, I had the opportunity to observe him as a patient afflicted with *Psychopathia sexualis*. I know of another case in which boys, while playing, were measuring their penises. I am not unaware of how many conversations boys hold about erection, etc.

above all else, the morals of the age-mates are worth diligently examining. Let parents be cautious in the selection of these, for often a man's entire fate depends on them. Youthful familiarity should be with those about whose probity and good morals the parents are assured. A true friend, an honest and forthright man who enjoys the young man's complete trust, may proffer the best preventative remedy. It is necessary to communicate to the youth certain anatomical ideas, and I do not understand why mankind, having searched through so much knowledge, would completely neglect an understanding of his own self. I think that the dignity and seriousness of the genital function ought to be communicated to the youth and that natural history, in particular the botanical, ought to be turned to this purpose. Sexual life can be first laid out for the young man in study of the sexual system of plants,[hh] then gradually, when he is older, it can be developed through the animal kingdom, beginning with the lowest classes. The tutor should select excerpts for himself from all of natural history and from these explain life's individual functions beginning with the lowest classes.[ii] He should communicate to the young man the development of each function in the higher orders. Nevertheless, he should not depict the sexual function in excessive detail, but should ensure that he arouse in the young man a desire for understanding and knowledge, but not curiosity. I confess that such instruction is difficult and that a learned man is needed who is prudent, serious, and of good morals so that fantasy is not excessively excited nor sexuality, yet sleeping, (*Geschlechtlichkeit*) be

---

hh. See the opening of this work: Development of the sexual system in animals and plants.

ii. Oken, *Naturgeschichte für alle Stände*. Virey, *Histoire naturelle du genre humain*.

stimulated. But in our own time, when there is such a waste of expenditure spent on futile matters, such as expecting children to speak ten languages and that they be taught all the arts to an artist's level of perfection, it will be right and fitting to impart something about care and expense for such a very serious issue. As for adults, this is not the place to trace out the laws for them concerning the sexual impulse; I only think they ought to be warned that one who detects in himself the analogous symptoms of *Psychopathia sexualis* should abstain not only from intercourse itself but from every form of excitement—kisses, sexual conversations, etc. The brain and genital system hold themselves as though at two poles, united by a Voltaic chain (if you will allow the term). Since when one of these is in a state of arousal, the other shares in the feeling. For this reason, an arousal of fantasy is so harmful for a person in whom the genital system is already compromised. Thus, intercourse should be moderate and suited to each individual, not premature and not prolonged beyond a certain age. For, as in a woman when the menses fall silent and her entire productive life stops, so in a man, a certain time comes when the vegetative life wanes throughout the whole body and the genital system is less supported by adequate powers for the purpose of exercising its function. Also pertinent here is the preconceived opinion of many who conclude that intercourse is a necessity because of a man's repeated erections. But I remind them that these depend no less on an irritated weakness and most often torture one afflicted with *tabes dorsalis*.

Radical Therapy

Since radical therapy can occur only within the first stage of *Psychopathia sexualis*, in explaining this therapy, I had envisioned only this first stage and omit that later therapy for *tabes dorsalis* that is sought in particular pathologies. For in the treatment of this horrendous disease, I would only be able to transcribe what has been said by others, since I lack experience and have never had the opportunity to observe the healing of true and confirmed *tabes dorsalis*.

I hope for the greatest usefulness from this therapy, which I will dare to explain more fully, in every case in which the effect of *Psychopathia sexualis* is spread through every organ and system but where the level of affliction has not passed beyond certain limits.

This therapy is indicated only when the genital system is weakened and truly exhausted and if in the genital sphere a weakness shows itself either as an irritation or as a true numbness and if the remaining systems—that of the nerves as much as of the veins and muscles—labor under an increased irritation, whether receptive or excitable—in short, when even the sphere supporting vegetative life succumbs to this evil.

This therapy is rendered questionable and put into doubt by that vital state when the sensitive and motor faculties begin to be extinguished in certain areas and when an excited vascular system demonstrates that the harmony of all the organs and systems is already damaged.

The conditions that absolutely forbid our therapy are an exhausted vital weakness, totally reduced functioning of sensation and motor skills, daily increasing atrophy, hectic fever, and destruction of certain noble organs. In such cases, it is necessary to resort to a vital cure in order that we excite the failing strength of the patient and revivify the weakened body. Our remedies for *Psychopathia sexualis* should respond to several indications: to control irritation of the sexual system, which always causes a new humoral dispensation; to strengthen the sexual system; to control an elevated vascular system; to hinder congestions or, if already present, to remove them; to extend the functions of the vegetative life—digestion and assimilation; to hold back profuse secretions but stimulate those that are hampered; to return to normal excretions; to bolster the muscular system that serves the vegetative life as much as the animal life; and, finally, to elevate the receptivity of the patient's sense-bearing life.

Such remedies must contain so many diverse properties with the result that they produce what we want. They should at the same time be anaphrodisiac and a soothing anti-inflammatory, both a tonic solvent and astringent, even narcotic. Moreover, such remedies culled from the pharmacologic treasury that satisfy conditions that are clearly opposed to themselves, I leave to the efforts of learned doctors. For I believe, and indeed any rational doctor not seized by a preconceived notion will agree with me, that in the vast pharmacological field no remedy bestowed with these properties is found and certainly mixing remedies with differing indications is as much harmful as foolish. I am not ashamed as a doctor to admit to the insufficiency both of the entire pharmacopeia of Europe and of formulas made with the greatest skill for liberally carrying out these indications; rather, my spirit moves me to offer a bold opinion: pharmaceutical remedies, unless selected with the utmost care, in *Psychopathia sexualis* contribute more harm than good. Nevertheless, this is not cause for despair because even if the pharmaceutical art forsakes the doctor, kindly nature provides us with a remedy, which we have before our eyes every day, is never lacking, and is of no cost. If we apply it shrewdly and intelligently on *Psychopathia sexualis*—at least in the first stage together with the psychological and lifestyle treatments—we may be able to destroy the seed of the disease and restore health. My colleagues will smile secretly if, when asked about my secret, I extol with highest praise

cold water as a directed remedy[jj][29] for this disease. The reasons
that convinced me of the greatest efficacy of cold water, I derived
not solely from direct observation and about which I myself have
knowledge. ("What remarkable experience can be demanded of a
junior doctor and, oh, how many cases of this type are given over
to the neophyte for observation!" I hear my opponents exclaim.
And however much I have been engaged in this question over very
many years, nevertheless, I must admit, if my sense of conviction
solely relied on this basis, it would be weakened enough and could
not be supported by strong arguments.) But almost every auxil-
iary of science, through which the elements of medicine are held
together, offers arguments that defend my thesis.

First, I will now demonstrate how highly valuable is the power of
cold water in the human organism, both in one that is healthy and
diseased. If we consult the chemical art, we are taught that water is
composed of the two elements oxygen and hydrogen and is found
in almost every foreign fluid and also those able to be excreted. (In
the process of respiration, water—or, at any rate, part of it—is dissolved; oxygen is expended in the exchange of venous blood from
arterial blood during its production; hydrogen is dispelled in every
secretion and excretion—urine, saliva, sweat.) Hydrogen and oxygen then are elements of every body, those in both the vegetable
and animal kingdoms; every organ of the human body consists for
the most part of these elements; and thus water shows the greatest
affinity with the human body.

Physiology teaches that water is the foundation of life and is especially necessary no less for infusoria than for vertebrate animals,
fungus, and the sensitive-plant [*mimosa pudica*].

jj. In so weit es Specifica giebt, wie Schwefel, Quecksilber u.s.w. [In so far as
there are *specifica*, such as sulfur, mercury, etc.]

In the functions of human life we find water everywhere as an agent. It is breathed in together with air impregnated with vapor and directly mixed with blood in the lungs. Then it suffuses through the skin and mucosal membrane by means of the villi of the lymphatic vessels and the veins in the vegetative sphere. In digestion, the production of both chyme and chyle require it. Nutrition (the secretion to organs) is not able to happen without it. Water serves for differing metamorphic processes in the dissolving of waste material. As transport, water moves this waste into vascular circulation, and the excretory organs by means of this liquid eliminate from the human organism those things that are depleted and useless for the body's restoration. And, thus, we find water in sweat, urine, saliva, etc.

A general pathology presents so many symptoms of disease in which the flow of water is not able to check itself. An overpowering amount of water in the human body favors chyme that is too thin, chyle that is endowed with the same character, badly mixed blood serum (or with an aqueous thinness), incomplete nutrition of all the organs (flaccid muscles), change in the cohesion of all the organs and an inclination to weakness, and overabundant secretions and excretions (and disturbed character to the secretions).

This pathological state easily produces an attendant accumulation of fluids, scurvy, excessive discharge of fluid, and dysentery, which is clearly obvious to every reader.[30] The contrary condition, a diminished amount of water in the human organism, produces the opposite state of the system—namely, chyme and chyle that are thick and because of this constipation there are obstructions in the lymphatic system and in the portal venous system. Blood itself tends rather to coagulate and is more plastic. The cohesion of all the organs is increased, and reverse metamorphosis is carried out more difficultly, since nature is not able to dissolve a material that is deprived of all organic traces. I should not believe incorrectly that irritable scrofula, an excess of abdominal fluid, acute fevers, and inflammations all owe the major part of their origin to this pathological state and in it find their explanation.

This is the right opportunity to demonstrate what sort of action is to be allotted to water in a weakened body by means of explanations about its efficacy in a healthy body and its relation to the production of illness, and also what place it is able to occupy in the pharmacological system. The effect of water varies according to its temperature, the place and means of application, the duration [of its application], and, in particular, the nature and character of the disease. At this point, only cold water requires discussion, since I have undertaken to defend its healthful effect, at least in the case of *Psychopathia sexualis*. A dynamic and material action combine in cold water when it is acting as a drug.

Dynamic action. When in contact with the human organism, water checks excessive swelling (a vital turgidity or sensitivity); it adds a greater power according to the principle that controls contraction (of the vascular and muscular systems). From this principle of contraction, we need to consider the first sign of water's effect, namely that unpleasant (almost painful) sensation—that sensation that we feel when we enter a cold bath. Our skin contracts; the temperature lowers at the place of contact; our vitality is truly augmented in our central organs, into which our blood rushes with the greatest force according to the obstructed urge to expand (positive pole) at the same time as there is an increased urge to contract (negative pole). But when cold water stops its influence, nature attempts to level out the disturbed equilibrium between the positive and negative poles, and, through increased vitality in the central organs and the simultaneous removal of any hindrance, the blood rushes into the peripheral organs, and from this come the secondary effects of cold water: a sense of heat, flushing, and finally a greater exaggeration in the functioning of the parts where we applied the cold water.[kk]

[Material action]. The material action of cold water easily stands out in my earlier statements. Chyme, chyle, lymph, and blood all become less thick; constipation in vascular circulation is released; secretions and excretions are more plentiful, etc.

From these things that I have mentioned it is readily apparent how much variety cold water offers as a drink, bath, injection, poultice, and plaster and how something so simple as water produces a variety of medical effects.

I could not abstain from these prefacing remarks if I dare to air my thesis: that cold water is indicated in *Psychopathia sexualis*, and no other drug can be found that is able to fulfill the [therapeutic] roles of cold water for this disease.

It would not be difficult to demonstrate that doctors in the most ancient of times already applied cold water as a remedy, but what would be the use in abundantly citing cases that were treated by means of cold water? Our book would increase in volume to no purpose since people today already proclaim water to be a panacea and doctors hold its effect to be useful for a great many illnesses. The followers of Kernius, from his time to the present, treat the greatest variety of diseased ulcers locally and solely with this remedy, and have convinced themselves that this action purifies and promotes health.[ll]

kk. Thus, cold water is used most correctly at the stage of eruptions in skin disease, in *typhus abdominalis*, etc.

ll. Chief of the hospital in the Vienna School.

Chief Physician Ratler, now deceased, was most successful in the treatment of contagious typhus.

I have seen eminent doctors in hospitals in Vienna, Geneva, London, Padua, and St. Petersburg apply cold poultices with the greatest success in exanthematic diseases[31] of the first stage (if the skin eruption was later) and typhoid fever.[mm] In gastric fevers and various conditions of the alimentary tubes and of the vegetative life (of differing characters) cold water as a drink performs the duty of a remedy. Among men of all races, cold water, especially taken in the morning, is a purging anti-inflammatory. Experience indicates that cold water is not only one of the remedies that loosen or diminish plasticity but it even assigns it a place among the remedies that are both tonic and for the increasing of plasticity. Certainly, there is no dispute that cold baths during summer increase a body's strength in weakened, emaciated patients. As an astringent it has a place in the advancement of medical binding. What is better than cold water on recent mechanical injuries, a wound, or a contusion? What is more in use? To what doctor has the opportunity been lacking for its application in cases of dysentery?

I believe, therefore, that I have sufficiently demonstrated that cold water is able to satisfy treatments that are directly opposed and that its use allows for many kinds of modifications. In *Psychopathia sexualis*, where the nature of the disease demands at one point depressive treatments, then ones that inflame, here ones that weaken, and there those that strengthen, what corresponds more to our wishes than a remedy that satisfies indications that are openly opposed and that in the hand of a learned and reasonable doctor fulfills the function of so many and such drugs? Last, I believe it is possible to affirm that it has not escaped the notice either of Priessnitz or many other celebrated doctors who

mm. Mylius.

are tireless in the practice of hydrotherapy that, in fact, healing is achieved with the sole aid of cold water. I myself have very often had the opportunity of observing the convalescence of a patient and then finally his restoration to health, but I myself have not followed that path.[32]

Since that time when my entire mind was occupied with this disease, I discovered the answer as to why practitioners of hydrotherapy have dared to treat diseases showing themselves under the most different forms and why in these diverse diseases, for which cold water seemed never to have been indicated, a worsened state so rarely followed [its use]. For so many patients who seek hydropathic approaches, *Psychopathia sexualis* seems to me to occupy a conspicuous place among the contributory causes, and often gushes forth from that font to which a cold, heredity, etc., is attributed. It seems easy to understand that a remedy suitable for an original disease cannot lack a beneficial effect for a secondary disease that was either aroused or maintained by the earlier one, and, in this way, many unaided healings have become clear to me. I would not have dared offer this opinion except that through a painstaking examination of wealthy patients I found that *Psychopathia sexualis* was almost always lurking or advanced. Its therapeutic usefulness in attendant diseases of the psychopathy is certainly a strong argument for this remedy's necessity for this disease itself. Therefore, cold water holds the first place among all remedies for this disease. Together with the psychological and lifestyle regimens it can destroy the disease at its first stage and remove its harmful effects on the human body, whereby it happens that the causal therapy happily achieves the end that it had set for itself.

Palliative therapy is in two situations of some account and ranking: (1) if the doctor has already tried in vain every drug and the disposition of the system and of the higher organs, and a later development of the [disease's] stages all render the approved remedy (cold water) more uncertain; (2) if dangerous symptoms of a unique character arise and demand emergency treatment. This would now be the place to survey the individual symptoms of the disease and explain their treatment, but it rarely occurs that a radical remedy does not respond to this indication, and then it is for the doctor to select each of the remedies and adapt them to each case. For that reason an explanation seems unnecessary to me. But there is, as well, a stronger reason that stops me from giving a complete particular description of the palliative treatment. Yet against my basic premise, an idea perhaps seizes my reader that he is treating himself as a patient and that, if he takes a half-bath and drinks much water, is able to go without a doctor. Indeed, water alone, without the lifestyle regimen and psychological treatment, may exert a healthful power, but in *Psychopathia sexualis* it neither helps nor harms, and the disease advances further.

It is therefore for the doctor to select the remedy indicated by the unique requirements and to prescribe a complete cure. The more in our age that self-treatment has become so common, like a priest performing a public duty, and because any old woman engages in conversation about medicine and a patient subjects medical formulas to his own examination, all the more carefully do I believe that every special palliative therapy should be avoided. Moreover, I repeat again and again that there is nothing more fatal, nothing more harmful in this disease than someone treating himself and by wasting time he makes his return to health more difficult, in fact impossible.

A doctor is necessary in such cases; without exception he is necessary. Let him be a true and sincere friend, enjoy complete trust, and certainly he will not lack aid in the restoring of health.

Secondary Diseases

In the preceding chapter I demonstrated the connection of the genital system with the organs and systems, and I set out the disease's effect in various areas. But in that chapter I looked at this only in order to instruct how *Psychopathia sexualis* makes the human organism inclined to so many diseased conditions and serves in developing these. It will be necessary at this point to enumerate the diseases that follow upon *Psychopathia sexualis* and explain their origin. Granted that I enumerated the three stages of *Psychopathia sexualis* in the part on prognosis, in my entire study I have only an account of the first stage, while omitting the later stages—attendant paralysis, wasting and exhaustive paralysis, which I encompass under the name *tabes dorsalis*. By no means does *tabes dorsalis* necessarily seize on the habit of onanism, even if it is exercised for an extended period. But there are countless other evils that follow incompletely cured *Psychopathia sexualis* or its first stage according to differences in age, sex, temperament, bodily constitution, habits, or its inclination to one or another system. I believe it is possible for my opinion to be proved by the following arguments:

1. *Tabes dorsalis* is no doubt a rather rare disease. But *Psychopathia sexualis* creeps far and wide through the human race. So, if *tabes dorsalis* must certainly follow upon *Psychopathia sexualis*, it would occur more frequently.
2. *Tabes dorsalis* also owes its origin to other causes,[nn] such as excessive strain of the extremities and hemorrhoids in the large intestine. It comes on suddenly during puberty and follows serious diseases during their recovery.
3. Misuse of coitus, especially premature intercourse or that which is too often repeated, offers the closest analogue to *Psychopathia*

nn. See Lallemand, "Des pertes seminales involontaires."

sexualis in its effect on the human organism, and only rarely may it lead to *tabes dorsalis*.

4. Observation at the bedside of patients has taught me that abstention from the accustomed vice over a rather extended period is sufficient already for the termination of a great many symptoms of the disease and for guarding against the expression of *tabes dorsalis*.

5. Many new patients, who as boys between the years of five and ten were given over to onanism, nevertheless may have remained safe from *tabes* but various other diseases were in evidence, whose direct connection with *Psychopathia sexualis* or their development from this disease is most easily deduced.

Those who believe it is not possible to say the word "onanism" without *tabes dorsalis* also coming to mind err, and err very greatly. *Tabes dorsalis* is a true secondary disease of *Psychopathia sexualis* that follows it under certain conditions, and the causes for its development depend more on the individual character than the span of time during which a man indulged in this vice. Often the repeated vice in one man does not produce *tabes*, while in another man this horrifying disease follows on a rarely repeated onanism. The cases in which *Psychopathia sexualis* ends in *tabes dorsalis* will be evident from what follows.

In the attendant diseases I will venture to set forth a sort of system, and will treat them according to age, sex, and temperament, as these differences of the vital state favor other diseases being produced from this source.

Age

A newborn infant is free from *Psychopathia sexualis*, but already at the second stage of infancy, after the eruption of the milk teeth, the first signs may be detected. I scarcely believe that onanism is evident before the first teeth erupt, but, rather, it begins between the first and second stages of dentition, most particularly at the seventh year up to the tenth. I have had the opportunity of observing this vice in younger boys, which became evident under the guise of nighttime bed-wetting. Dentition has almost no connection with the sexual psychopathy; rather, it even prevents its development. While the formative force [*vis plastica*] of life energetically engages in this process, sexuality withdraws more and is lulled by a deep sleep. Later, when animal life flourishes more during the day, then it germinates. Scrofula, ringworm, and especially types of diseases that are attributed to the development of the body have a certain causal connection with onanism, of which they are the cause, the effect, or the coeffect.

Contagious skin diseases are in no direct relationship. Certain types of impetigo, such as herpes or scabies, ought to be attributed among the etiological causes of the disease. As for fevers, at least typhoid and pituitary fever have a connection. The remaining fevers are, at any rate, sustained though this disease; they become more long lasting, do not preserve their regular form, and become irregular (the change of gastric fever into nervous is supported). At the age of young adulthood, the more rapid development of the genitals arouses sexual love and entices the youth to intercourse.[oo] Concerning the syphilitic virus, I have noted from a few observations that *Psychopathia sexualis*, in dissipating the sexual life, encourages the infection and renders the attack of the venereal disease of longer duration or more perilous.

oo. If the vitality is not broken too much, intercourse, in truth especially with an honest and upstanding love, is able to heal a psychopathy of a more recent origin, at any rate in the first stage.

The efficacy of cold water on syphilis confirms my opinion. Young adulthood encourages inflammations of the noble organs, especially the lungs, brain, heart, and intestinal tubes, and *Psychopathia sexualis* occupies almost the first place in the disposition toward these conditions, not only in a young man but even in an adult man. At any rate, depending on the different condition, it may afflict the brain with apoplexy, the lungs with atrophy, the chylopoetic system with hemorrhoids, or the lymphatic system with scrofula. At the age of male adulthood this psychopathy rarely shows itself. If a man previously indulged in it, now its effect, because of the autocracy of life, gradually becomes effaced, and on account of the greater vigor of life and the greater harmony of all the functions at this age, secondary diseases arising from this source happen more rarely. But if the disease persists, given that the mental faculties have reached the height of development, the various attendant diseases emerge into the light: the animal and vegetative life are afflicted. These conditions unexpectedly slither forth, and they will be the more serious by how much less they arouse the attention of either the patient or doctor at their onset. Many of these conditions that owe their start to *Psychopathia sexualis* are typically attributed to the constitution of the body. Experience has taught me that lazy eye,[pp] loss of vision, and various epilepsies, especially those simulating lapses, "Saint Vitus' dance," spasms, and paralyses,[qq] are all born from *Psychopathia sexualis* through a direct connection at the outset. In individuals suffering

pp. There was a man, thirty-eight years old, working at a public job, in whom lazy eye suddenly developed. He was blessed with a laudable constitution, always in good health. He confessed to me under an accurate examination that he never had engaged in intercourse but had always satisfied his lust by the rubbing of his member with the help of women.

qq. A case that I related in my tract on ferruginous waters.

from oversensitivity there are various pains—rheumatism and face pain[rr] come into view for which this psychopathy contributed not a little in terms of production and maintenance. All of these diseases are more unique to the wealthy, in whom the aberration of the sexual instinct certainly occurs more frequently than among the poor. Familiar pains come into evidence at home, less so in the hospital, and always in association with an apathy of the entire sexual life. Women afflicted with such a disease are for the most part sterile.

Cold water is recommended among the remedies of the first order against these afflictions, and Priessnitz owes a large part of his glory to the efficacy of this remedy in conditions flowing forth from such a source (*ps. s.*).[33]

Abdominal plethora with a host of abdominal ailments (hemorrhoids, constipation, hydrops, jaundice, arthritis) and so many mental wanderings (what and how will be made known later) gush out jointly from this source.[34] I believe that old age is more immune from the secondary conditions of *Psychopathia sexualis*, for if the life of a man afflicted with this disease has lasted up to this period, certainly the autocracy of life has terminated all harmful effects. The evils particular to this period of the disease, and even sudden death, I believe ought to be attributed to other causes, among which a place is to be assigned to the extended strain on the sexual faculty.

Temperament

Certainly temperament offers a great variation in the genesis of diseases resulting from *Psychopathia sexualis*; therefore, a few

rr. I saw secondary gonorrhea in a man of forty-eight years, that had lasted for twenty years and was accompanied with face pain; when the face pain healed, it suddenly disappeared.

words concerning temperament and its meaning seem necessary to me. Every doctor may agree with me that rarely in the sick does such a temperament become evident as is described in general pathology. From this, the opinion has arisen that rarely is a pure temperament to be found but, rather, one that is mixed as if composed from two. This opinion does not seem to correspond to the truth, for what is temperament other than a unique mode of life that, from its first origin, life places in each person? Any mode is a particular form of existence that comes into being openly through certain fixed signs; thus, I am not able to grasp in my thoughts how life can present differing forms that are sometimes in opposition to one another at the same time. Mixed temperaments, as many understand these, rarely come into view at the same time and allow another, easier explanation. Temperament, as a unique mode of life, includes the mental life as much as the physical, both of which can be modified by external causes, so that another character is impressed on [the original] one. Therefore, it can happen that physical life (constitution) undergoes a change differently from the mental, which is more variable and more subject to the power of external causes. From this emerges a "mixed" temperament, if the mental life provides a character different from the physical, which depends more on the constitution and, being less subject to variations, is more consistent. Experience confirms this change in temperament: a newborn almost lacks a temperament, and it would be a hard task to settle on a diagnosis for something barely hatched from the uterus. An infant and youth enjoy more of a sanguine temperament (the phlegmatic being indicative of disease at this point in life). At adulthood he becomes choleric, which is sometimes overtaken by a melancholic temperament, and an old man is a pure phlegmatic.

This circuit of temperaments corresponds to the development of the body: at the most tender age receptivity is boundless, and there is no reaction. Gradually, the reactive impulse is augmented, and at the culmination of life both powers enjoy the same level. Then, at a more advanced age, receptivity recedes and reaction is at that point lively, until at last both are exhausted and lulled into the lethargic sleep of old age.

How often a disease, a suffering of the soul, or another cause is able to change a man's temperament! Surely, are not consumptives filled with a vain hope? Almost always the submelancholic are grim. *Psychopathia sexualis* penetrates into the temperament in a horrendous way: it robs a young man endowed with a sanguine temperament, as they say, of all hope and taints his senses and thoughts with a black color.[ss] Certainly, a sudden change in temperament cannot advance similarly in both the mental and physical life; for the physical mode of life emerges from the originary arrangement of the body, from the special laws of the body's development, as if under guiding principle of one or another of the systems. This way of life undoubtedly cannot be changed in a moment. Otherwise the situation has to do with the mental part of the temperament or the mode of life of the intellectual faculties, which can more easily be changed.

A child endowed with the greatest gifts of the mind who lacks all education will remain idle in this sphere and his temperament will be sanguine in relation to his body, but phlegmatic in relation to his mind. Habit most especially works in us (man is the supreme animal); from this it happens that if children often see their own

---

ss. The lassitude toward life unique to our age and its melancholic young men certainly acknowledge a fertile font in *Psychopathia sexualis*.

parents, teachers, or fellow students are angry, they themselves become choleric (mentally). From the foregoing, I venture to conclude that temperament consists of two elements—the physical and the mental, whose swift changes it is able to manage. The physical element includes the constitution, the physical condition—in a word, it is the means of material existence that shows itself with certain fixed signs. The combination of these signs produces in the physical temperament a more serious power for either animal or vegetative life. Thus, two cardinal physical temperaments are distinguished: the animal and the vegetative. In an animal temperament, either a life capable of sensation or one that is irritable holds sway; from this, the animal temperament divides into the sensitive (sanguine) and the irritable (choleric). Vegetative life is able to be very powerful in a doubled way: either the plastic force is superior, more elaborated, or it is inferior and the form of the plastic matter is restricted to the lymph. In this way, the vegetative temperament divides into the higher (melancholic) and lower (phlegmatic). The mental or immaterial element embraces every faculty of thinking and understanding, and these, when refined to the highest level of development, produce a choleric temperament, while their lack produces a phlegmatic one. A preponderance of the cognitive faculty (memory, imagination) creates a sanguine temperament, but an overabundance of the intellectual faculty (intelligence, judgment, reason) creates a melancholic one. Since the mental temperament is most easily changed, this classification cannot be definitive. For neither in the sanguine temperament is the intellectual faculty entirely missing nor in the cognitive temperament is the melancholic missing. Only in relation to the other faculty does it enjoy a lower level of development. The following schema gives an easier overview:

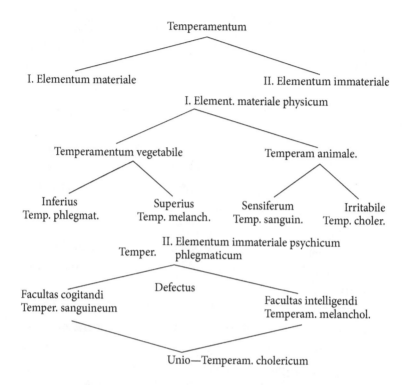

I seek pardon from the reader since I have allowed myself this digression from our path; but it could not be avoided in order to explain the causal connection between *Psychopathia sexualis* and its attendant diseases.

What was said in the preceding chapter about the effects of *Psychopathia sexualis* on the human organism, one who considers it well understands that since [the human] system is more developed, this harmful effect of *Psychopathia sexualis* must be felt most powerfully. I will treat the attendant diseases according to this classificatory schema, and, indeed, I will begin for logic's sake with the material element of the temperament. A man graced with a sanguine temperament is most easily afflicted with this psychopathy; oversensitivity (lack of toleration for stimuli) combined with strong sense perception favors the germination of the evil, supports the disease, and causes it to be recurring. It is even more dangerous if an immaterial sanguine element associates itself with this material sanguine element: the imagination being very powerful suddenly creates *Psychopathia sexualis* in its most restricted sense (mental onanism), which renders the disease most stubborn and highly detrimental to the patient. It makes every cure of the doctor useless, and there is little hope of removing the illness.[tt]

By what powers is medicine strong enough to subdue a heightened imagination, if the crippled will of the patient does not help the doctor?

Diseases attendant on *Psychopathia sexualis* in a sanguine physical temperament will be diseases in particular of the nervous system, especially neuroses (pains, epilepsy, etc.). Intermittent fevers, because of this, acquire an irregular abnormal type; other diseases such as rheumatism and chronic inflammations counterfeit an intermittent character.

In the sanguine physical temperament mixed with a sanguine mental one, *tabes dorsalis* is easily generated from *Psychopathia sexualis* if the following conditions accompany it: a longer duration of the illness, a weak constitution in the patient, many advanced diseases, no therapy or one that is inconsistent. Truly, if these conditions are missing, then, even if the patient is safe from *tabes dorsalis*, *Psychopathia sexualis* with a swift step changes

---

tt. From this, I explain why the disease is more difficult to heal in adolescence than in adulthood, than adults, why a more advanced age often spontaneously cures the disease, etc.

the sanguine temperament (mental) into a melancholic (mental) one.

The choleric temperament, the flower of development and the acme of human perfection, enjoys a greater vital strength and liveliness; it halts recurrence and results in a complete recovery of health.[uu] The effects of this disease, if it has lasted for a longer period, seek out the vascular and muscular systems. Every attendant disease shares an acute character, inflammation and fevers present a more remittent than intermittent type.

Especially in the choleric mental temperament, the intrusion of *Psychopathia sexualis* becomes noticeable, and it changes either into a sanguine mental type[vv] or a melancholic type. In this temperament, one may observe the relationship of *Psychopathia sexualis* to the psyche and physical nature (*physis*): the more it is seen in the one, the less in the other and vice versa.

The melancholic temperament is less subject to the psychopathy, seeing as both the physical and mental type do not occur either in childhood or young adulthood, and indeed at those ages it is a disease. In young adulthood, as we have already mentioned, it develops with the aid of this disease out of either a sanguine or choleric temperament. The attendant diseases will be, in particular, various disturbances coming from the derangement of the organs responsible for assimilation and nutrition (such as abdominal plethora, constipation, hemorrhoids, hydropes, etc.).

uu. Pertaining to this are the cases of those who have been subjected to this evil for a rather long time yet nevertheless enjoyed good health.

vv. I know a case of a forty-seven-year-old man who was addicted to masturbation in young adulthood; later on he suffered from *Psychopathia sexualis* in its most restricted sense (mental onanism) and changed from having a choleric (mental) temperament to a melancholic one. Previously, he had enjoyed extremely developed mental faculties, but then he began to complain, correctly, about the dullness of his synthetic faculties (memory, imagination, etc.).

The phlegmatic temperament (physical) occurs even in children. Therefore, it is susceptible to this disease on account of a lower vitality, which is engaged in a direct relation with sexuality, and that favors the germination and development of *Psychopathia sexualis*. Among the illnesses that follow on *Psychopathia sexualis* or develop at its intrusion, scrofula stands out (about which we have already discussed), as does worm infection, for the vegetative life when reduced to a lower level favors the development of worms, and finally epilepsy, etc., and many diseases that originate from the disposition of the chylopoetic system. If such a temperament (material element) forms an association with a phlegmatic temperament (immaterial element), then the failure of the entire intellect and weakening of memory renders every mental mode of healing more difficult.[ww] Cretinism offers a sad and vivid example of such an association. I have never seen such a patient without having uncovered the symptoms and effects of this evil in him. Because sexuality responds to the laws of nature, however lower the life is then all the more is sexuality in control, as in individuals whose psyche is lulled with an unending lethargy.

On Mental Diseases

It will be better if I study all such afflictions uniformly, because then their origin and the causal connection can be more easily understood.

Rarely is *Psychopathia sexualis* a direct cause of mental illnesses, but certainly through the soul it prepares a way for afflictions and

ww. In such a case, neglected upbringing always can be accused; for a newborn infant is almost always phlegmatic (mentally), and with the aid of education, at least, the mental faculties are developed.

sufferings in the generation of mental diseases. The mind refers everything that it ponders back either to the thing or to itself and desires what it perceives to be good and suitable for itself. But it avoids that which it ascertains is bad or repugnant. These pleasurable and distasteful sensations and the resulting desires and aversions, even the will's preference for good or bad (*Willensäusserung*), all obey the soul and acknowledge it as master. At the beginning, the sexual instinct monopolizes the whole attention of the mind, and then in due course [it monopolizes] every reflection of the will. *Psychopathia sexualis* itself, as an affliction of the soul, will be of a fugitive nature and yield its place as the functions again harmonize. Its descent becomes a true suffering of the soul when the lustful sensation is directed back to the steady center of the entire mind, around which almost every thought and the whole impulse of the will turns itself in a perpetual course.

Psychopathia sexualis as an affliction of the soul in the beginning and then later, as a pathology, supports the development of mental illness from different psychical temperaments. In the different temperaments that flow out from this disease (*Psychopathia sexualis*), moreover, various afflictions of the soul are found and aid in the development of mental diseases, especially shame and regret because of some error having been committed: in the sanguine [the affliction is] fear; in the choleric, terror. The effect of these afflictions differs according to type, to their strength and constancy through which they function. At the least, they harmonize because they excite the organs that control thought and volition with constant stimulation, and thus they support the various dispositions of the psyche. Experience at this point also confirms the law stated previously: the more the system is developed in the human organism, the more it becomes a partner in the harmful effects of *Psychopathia sexualis*. From this, it is evident what kind of disposition of the mind emerges from this source in the various psychical temperaments.

Mania or the diseased heightened activity of the primary powers of thought, perception, recall, and of combinatory thought is developed more in the choleric and sanguine types. In the choleric, the faculty governing thought and intelligence is raised to a higher level, while in the sanguine the faculty of thought in its normal state prevails. Insanity, that affliction in which the primary powers of thought are normal but those of understanding are diseased or the internal governance of thought is not able to be applied to these properly, is dominant in the choleric and melancholic. In the choleric both faculties are already naturally more refined, while in the melancholic the intellectual faculty is endowed with greater power and energy. From this, the mind's derangement develops with greater difficulty, but if it develops, it will be more serious, more steadfast, and more difficult to cure.

The types of insanity that draw their origin directly from *Psychopathia sexualis* are the impulse to kill oneself in melancholics and the inexplicable impulse for satisfying lust (nymphomania in women), which in all psychical temperaments associates itself with mental illness arising from *Psychopathia sexualis.*

Dementia, or that state in which all powers of cognition appear weakened and below normal, as subsequent to mania or insanity, occurs in every psychical temperament, but it appears out of *Psychopathia sexualis* especially in the phlegmatic temperament, in which already in a sane state all the intellectual faculties are less vigorous, lacking both energy and strength.

The soul, distracted by a variety of things, presents a type of diminished activity in the powers of thought (*Zerstreuheit*), which certainly may be observed in boys laboring under onanism. In these boys, the soul is seized in another direction (sexual), and the boy lives in dreams that are for the most part voluptuous, and he yields to the disease of his soul (the sexual impulse).

Psychopathia sexualis in its most strict sense (mental onanism) ought to be mentioned here as it renders the perceptive ability lame and incomplete due to the imagination's fantasies. The failure of memory produces forgetfulness, which can produce either idiocy or the failure of the combinatory faculty.

Neumann in such cases of dementia that appear from onanism recommends for girls the excising of the clitoris and for boys circumcision.[xx]

On Sex

Although throughout this book I have offered few words concerning how the disease differs in the feminine sex, according to the reasons mentioned in the preface, nevertheless, at this point necessity drives me to briefly explain the changes in the disease's effects according to sex. In men, the animal force predominates, in women the plastic. Man may be called almost an animal, woman a plant. The plastic force in a woman enjoys the highest level of development and, as an extension (providing nutrition beyond itself), embraces the whole life of a woman. In truth, with women the higher animal life withdraws and sensibility is conspicuous, but it is often united to hypersensitivity (an intolerance to stimulation), and her less developed irritability (reaction) lacks vim and vigor. Her whole anatomical structure effectively demonstrates the end and goal of feminine existence and pronounces this with vivid and clear signs, since the sequence of functions, solely unique to the weaker sex, sufficiently proves this. Her entire skeleton is

xx. *Spec. Pathologie und Therapie*, by Dr. Carl Georg Neumann, vol. 4, p. 474.

shaped in a different way; the organs of respiration and circulation are less developed while those of the abdominal cavity, especially the pelvic cavity, are superior; her voice is weaker and her thorax narrower and more flat; her pulse is weaker or faster (from her hypersensitivity); her bones and muscles are weaker, except for the lumbar and gluteal muscles. In the vascular system, the venous system predominates in a woman; in her nervous system, the pubic plexus and that of the genitals are more developed.

The genitals' structure places the duty assigned to a woman (productivity) beyond any doubt. The genitals of the feminine sex are situated inside and are hidden. They are protected by strong powers of reaction against violence from external forces. Their form is more complex and developed. The uropoetic system enjoys a unique excretory duct (which in a man serves a dual purpose: uropoetic and genital). The dignity and seriousness of this function in women is evident from the great flock of diseases that are produced from the deranged functioning of this system, while in men, if you exclude *Psychopathia sexualis*, there is no general illness that develops in the genital sphere without an external cause. Puberty in girls makes its assault with certain and fixed signs that are lacking in a young girl, and its function is evident: it maintains and prepares the entire genital sphere for activity and when it ceases indicates the local death of the sexual system.

The way of life or the temperament (physical) in women is vegetative. Therefore, the lower phlegmatic temperament rather than the higher melancholic one appears in them, more rarely still the sanguine, and rarest of all the choleric. In women the imaginative faculty excels, but the power of the intellect recedes, hence women enjoy an especially sanguine temperament relative to the immaterial element, and more rarely another type. Among the cognitive faculties, their sense of perception stands out, their ability to recall is weak, and the faculty of combinatory thinking is still less powerful. Therefore, women most infrequently excel with a keen genius, and, no matter how diligently they are instructed, they rarely produce great fruits of genius.

From these prefatory statements, it is adequately clear that the end goal of the feminine life is the propagation of the human race and the conservation of its stock; therefore, sexual life creates a center for the entire life in women. Certainly, every physiologist and obstetrician may concur with me on this matter, and the sad image of a girl unmarried at a more advanced age manifestly shows how nature punishes the unsatisfied destiny of a woman. But, if the sexual system occupies the first and principal place in a woman's life, why is it a wonder if *Psychopathia sexualis* seeks out most powerfully this system and, first of all, lays traps for it, while being less hostile to the rest of the systems and organs?

The fact that in children of the feminine sex onanism more rarely occurs than in boys finds an explanation in the position of the genitals, in the clothing of girls, and in their sense of chastity, which is never lacking in them. At the time of puberty, *Psychopathia sexualis* is even found in the weaker sex, and acknowledges as its cause her sexuality that is already developing according to the laws of nature. From this time, it cannot be doubted that even girls practice masturbation, though they especially love the fantasies of the imagination and hold themselves in an aroused state and are entertained by *Psychopathia sexualis* in its most restricted sense.[yy]

yy. At this point many things ought to be reported about its etiology, especially the sedentary life of wealthy girls, for the disease no doubt appears more rarely among maidservants and inhabitants of the countryside than among the wealthy and noble—this sedentary life lacks strong bodily movement and occupations that tire one out.

Wives certainly are safe from this disease, but if wealth or similar reasons have contracted the marriage and moral love for the husband and children is missing, or if the evil habit has held the girl for very many years and the sexual instinct has carried her away, then *Psychopathia sexualis* appears even in married women. It will be possible to offer another reason—if women are neglected by their husbands with only a few years of marriage having passed and the other opportunity for fulfilling the sexual instinct is missing. At a more advanced age, when the sexual life ceases in a woman, this *Psychopathia sexualis* suddenly dissipates and its traces remain in the excessive love for dogs or cats indulged in by every old woman.

Those things that follow on *Psychopathia sexualis* vary according to the age of the female patient, the duration of the disease, the repetition of the vice, her constitution and bodily arrangement—in short, according to the individual. They become most strongly evident in the sexual system of women so that the menses become irregular or premature (irritated) or late, or labored and painful, or her menses are easily delayed or suppressed at the slightest opportunity. The flow of blood is anomalous or too much or too little. The blood itself is strange in its quality, either too plastic or coagulated, or in the place of this appears a clear mucous or some clear-formed matter, which points out that the excretory genital system is afflicted by some chronic irritation or catarrh. Even though a woman should have been destined most powerfully for the propagation of the human race, she would be involuntarily driven to coitus, and women are found who refuse the embrace of a man (this weakness is an indirect consequence of too much excitation) or who are provoked by an immoderate lust (this irritative weakness is a characteristic sign of *Psychopathia sexualis*). The inability of a woman to engage in coitus either because of genital pain (*erethism*) or from a deformity (that may also be a consequence of *Psychopathia sexualis*) ought to be diverted. Sterility is explained either as a result of a deformity or from her weakness, since a woman should contribute seed to the arrangement, or from a justifiable lack of a dynamic between the man and woman.

How often *Psychopathia sexualis* is a cause of sterility seems to me to be proved by the fact that it appears more among civilized and educated peoples than among the uncultured, more among city dwellers than among those in the country, and more among the rich than among the poor.

Psychopathia sexualis is especially able to bring about sterility if a woman has indulged in this vice for a long time or if her husband has been corrupted by this disease for a rather long period of time. At any rate, men with an excessive sex drive lack the ability of generation. In relation to birth, the troubles are various that vex a woman, which are caused by and maintained not a little by *Psychopathia sexualis*: dullness to the pains of birth (the animal life being already previously exhausted or reduced to a lower level), hemorrhage (the plastic force failing, vascular tension broken), retention of the placenta (muscular paralysis of the uterus), lack of emotion (irritation of the nervous system), etc.

Lochia has a function analogous to the menses, and they are almost proxies for each other. The secretion of milk from this cause undergoes not small disturbances, and various childbed illnesses (puerperal fever, metroperitonitis, puerperal mania, etc.) acknowledge in this (*ps. s.*) their formative cause.

Even in the human egg, *Psychopathia sexualis* exerts its pernicious power. For when the plastic force of the uterus has been previously destroyed and animal life seized with an irritative weakness, neither the fetus nor its covering is shaped according to nature's norm. Following birth and later in the woman's sexual life, various afflictions appear that have a certain causal connection with the disease here described, such as inflammation or hardening of the orifices of the uterus, degeneration of these or of the uterus (*scirrhus*), polyps, hydropes, tilting of the uterus, or prolapse accompanied with transposition, etc. By no means do I think that I rashly offer my opinion that in a woman her very sexual life especially shares in the effects of *Psychopathia sexualis*.

Pathological Anatomy

Today, pathological anatomy sheds so much light over the vast field of disease, which was previously hidden under a mysterious veil and glutted with hypotheses, that it would be my duty to say a few words sensibly concerning those things that the autopsy of cadavers teaches about the organic products of *Psychopathia sexualis*. But such a project is useless because experience eludes me, for genital organs marked with a pathological anatomy are not worthy of that attention that is accorded the other organs. Anatomical sectioning of the genitals is altogether neglected or is carried out in a cursory and incidental way, as the most distinguished Lallemand already warns in his preeminent book on diseased pollutions. At the dissection table often a history of the diseases or case discussions are lacking, and the hospital doctor, not knowing the entirety of the patient's life that has gone before, pays very little attention to this material, and the doctor in a private practice is held back from this duty due to his excessive busyness. Well-written histories of diseases are becoming rarer these days, and I have so far been unable to win the confidence of my colleagues such that I could have collected abundantly these histories that are able to explain accurately this material that is so difficult. How is it possible that I, a novice doctor, dare to study material that is only proper for men to study who are engaged in pathology and when the genius and perseverance is needed of men like Lallemand, Laennec, Corvisart, Meckel, Skoda, or Rokitansky!

Therefore, I leave this material for a later time when I will treat specifically pathological anatomy and I hope that these first fruits of my study will raise the reputation of my work and make possible the opportunity of observing many cases.

I think that it is worthwhile, nevertheless, on account of the rarity [of these] to add a brief case history of a patient whom I have known since his most tender infancy and in whom I had the opportunity to observe the descent of the entire disease, whom I myself treated as a doctor, and whose pathological dissection laid open for me the state of all his organs and systems.

> *Psychopathia sexualis* in the first stage under the form of masturbation; irritation of the spine forming at once an exudate into the spinal cavity with paralysis of the upper and lower extremities, clonic spasms in the involuntary and voluntary muscles, and finally a spontaneous hanging dislocation of the right femur.

During the course of the disease, lasting for eighteen months,[35] there was associated tuberculosis of the lungs, kidneys, and intestines; bedsores; fistulae and innumerous fistular ulcers: in short, the entire diagnosis resounds with:[36]

"Noli Me Tangere"

Mauritius S. . . . , a young man of eighteen years, of Jewish origin, who later embraced the Christian faith, already as a child excelled with a premature sharpness of the mind. On account of the generosity and kindness of his soul, throughout the entire short course of his life, he was loved greatly by his parents and by everyone who knew him. At first, he was dedicated to his letters and studies,[zz] then sought a military career, and with highest success executed his military service in such a way that the testimony of his professors designated him among the outstanding young men at that place. In his family, we found that the nervous system was preeminent: his father in adulthood suffered a sudden apoplexy; his mother for a rather long period of time was seized with a mental illness and held in a hospital for the insane;[aaa] hydrocephalus killed his younger brother in his earliest infancy, while his older brother, excelling most particularly with a sharp intellect, with the greatest constancy is dedicated to Minerva and holds out comfort and hope for their mother.

I do not know whether it was in the gymnasium or later in the military institution that he became given over to onanism, but it can be assumed, since already as a boy he presented clear symptoms of *Psychopathia sexualis*. His premature puberty and way of life certainly contributed much to developing the diseased seed. The attack of the disease itself sufficiently indicated its origin from this source, like a serpent afflicting all his organs and systems, making every therapy vain, even harmful. He was always healthy, up to the sixteenth year of life; from that time, which he passed in the military academy, he began to grow sick and to labor with pains at the nape of his neck and forehead; at the beginning he was treated homeopathically. Since the evil was increasing daily, he was transferred from the homeopathic hospital into an allopathic one. Even at that place, where anti-inflammatory methods were called

zz. At the gymnasium, where masturbation was so widespread that hardly a boy could be found who was not tainted by this vice.

aaa. She was completely cured in the eminent institute for the insane of Dr. Görgen in Vienna.

more widely into use, all were exerted to no avail, for daily the disease was growing worse.

From the point when I had the opportunity to observe him together with a colleague of mine, that dearest of friends Dr. Preuss, complete paralysis in his leg and arm had already developed, and at the same time consuming pains, concentrating in the region of his nape, troubled the patient. Supposing there was an underlying irritative condition of his spine, we called into use an anti-inflammatory method—pumpkins on the neck, alternate remedies (emetic tartar with ipecac and cut with a dose of opium).

When this therapy proved to neither benefit nor harm him, we changed the treatment and anticipated a favorable effect from strychnine. Even though this alkaloid material was administered most cautiously and at the lowest dose, nevertheless there were sudden clonic seizures, especially in the flexor muscles of the leg, which then caused his leg to move up toward his thigh, with the result that both legs formed two very sharp angles while at the same time there were spasms in other areas, in his abdomen, heart, etc. This abnormal position of his lower extremities was seen at the onset only as long as the attack lasted, then increasingly it troubled the patient every day until it remained constant.

As help, the most celebrated doctors in Vienna (Vering, Pronz) were called in for consultation, and they indicated that the disease arose from something exuded into his vertebral canal. This extrusion owed its origin to neglected rheumatism (treated homeopathically) of the vertebral column's ligaments. A method was put into effect for exciting the celiac system and supporting reabsorption (an infusion of senna alternating with an infusion of arnica flowers). This therapy changed nothing in the patient's state, but as his strength diminished daily, emaciation appeared throughout his whole body. A new doctor (the most eminent Bischoff) was called in to help and declared that the disease *tabes dorsalis* had developed, and, in accord with his reasoning, light healing nutrients—anti-inflammatories (oil, whey, milk)—were applied for a rather long period. The patient's condition remained always the same, but the spasms were tormenting him more frequently every day, and they were of longer duration. We were forced to abandon this method of cure, thoroughly educated by these erring attempts, and we tried mercury in the form of an ashy unguent at the lowest dosage, but the symptoms of mercury poisoning (a metallic flavor, excessive saliva) becoming visible on the fifth day forbade further continuation of this remedy. I pass in silence over the other remedies that in the present case were called into use to no avail. They offered nothing, and they only worsened the state of the patient. Of all these only cherry oil, like paregoric, is worthy of mention because it alleviated his pain for the moment and mitigated the spasm. The mother of the poor man, no longer deceived as to the outcome of the disease, took consultation in order to come to a decision concerning the patient's fate—to abstain from every therapy and abandon him to nature. I, myself, joined to this family by friendship, affirmed this advice, as what hope for therapy shines in such a case where art and science have abandoned the doctor and where the remedy behaves like a poison?

In truth, under such negative treatment the patient's condition seemed better; the paralysis of his arms ceased, motion was returned, and also one of his lower extremities showed traces of sensitivity, so much so that hope shone out that the patient might undertake a trip to the baths of Poesthen. But this improvement was fictitious. The patient's strength was consumed. Hectic fever attacked, making every attempt at a trip impossible, but this still offered some good as it gave the patient a certain hope of recovering his health and lightened his death, which finally followed after twenty-two months that were filled with greatest pain. Because the nature of this disease is a matter of dispute, experience alone confirmed for me this prescription: "*Noli me tangere.*" It will be better to treat more fully the autopsy, which does not deceive a viewer, than to further pursue the course of this disease that moved all those who ever saw the patient to the greatest pity.

The shape of his body was diminished to half (since his leg made an angle with his thigh), and there was general emaciation, gangrenous bedsores on his sacral region, and quite numerous fistulae from around the anus all the way to the pubic region. There was such a folding of the shin up to femur so that they formed almost a perpendicular line; this contraction was so violent that it lasted sixteen hours after his death, and in the posterior femoral region there was observed to be rotting in the flesh. The brain was slightly soft, the rest natural. His lungs were covered thickly with both solitary and aggregate tuberculosis, with ulcers and various pleurisies, and the bronchi were blocked with a viscid mucous. The liver was normal. There was catarrh of the intestines and exposed solitary tuberculosis in the region of the Brunner glands. His spleen was softer, the kidneys obstructed with tuberculosis, the bladder afflicted with catarrh, and his atrophied testicles were smaller. There was an intrusion of the smaller blood vessels into the medulla oblongata, a serous exudate into the entire dorsal cavity beyond the pia mater, a pustule discharge into the subcutaneous cellular tissue in the most diverse places of the body, and the glenoid cavity was filled with a pus-like mass. The head of the femur had completely dislocated from its cavity.

From this I conclude that in such a state of ruin of all the diverse organs a doctor has no power, and only a rather swift end is to be desired for the patient. The disease seems to me to have its origin from the rheumatism of his system of ligaments that, without the help of the medical arts (homeopathically), attacked his spine (disposed to infections from the progressed state of *Psychopathia sexualis*), which led to an underlying inflammatory condition that immediately produced a true exudate. From this early paralysis of the upper and lower extremities spasms proceeded from the irritation of the nervous system—a characteristic symptom of *Psychopathia sexualis* and incompatible with therapy. During its further course, tuberculosis in the lungs and a purulent infusion in the subcutaneous membrane added themselves. The bedsores require no special explanation in an illness of twenty-two months. The lively vital power of his young adulthood, the patient's robust constitution, the lack of advanced diseases, the immunity of his intestines and liver that were only affected at the latest stage—all these explain the continuation of the disease for so many months, for his appetite was strong all the way up until death, his bowels normal, his evacuation only most difficult because of the development of paralysis in his rectal intestine. The uropoetic system was lively enough, for his periodic retention of urine owed its origin only to the spasms. The fluorescence of rot arose from the repeated and violent contraction of the thigh's flexors (especially the muscles: internal iliac, the psoas major and minor, and the pectineus were blamed)—and the abnormal position of the lower leg in relation to the upper thigh because of the contraction of the leg's flexors (muscles: bicipital, gracile, semimebranous, and semitendinous). We recognize that the originary causes of this disease are the preponderant nervous system in the entire family of the patient, their Oriental origin, and especially *Psychopathia sexualis*. The opportunistic causes are the cooling and inappropriate homeopathic treatment, which supplied the horrific development of this disease.

The sad history of this disease adequately shows that in addition homeopathy is able to cause harm, especially during the first stage of *Psychopathia sexualis*. If the disease shows itself as a spinal irritation, then doctors should be mindful of providing anti-inflammatory therapy and may judge a homeopathic (negative) treatment in such cases to be most strenuously disparaged.

Appendix

(Translation from German by Maya Vinokour)

Anonymous. "Review: *Psychopathia sexualis*," *Monthly Journal of Medical Science* 5 (1845): 494–96.[1]

Psychopathia Sexualis. Auctore Henrico Kaan, *Medico Ruthenico et Doctore Medicinae Vindobonnensi, &c.* 8vo.; pp. 124. Lipsiae: 1844.
(*Mental Sexual Disease. By* Henry Kaan, M.D., &c.)

This work, notwithstanding the extraneous matter which it contains, is on the whole, creditable to the author; and this can be said of few of the many books, pamphlets, and papers that have been printed on the revolting subjects of which it treats.

It consists of two parts. The first part contains much that is irrelevant to therapeutics, though they are professedly the great aim of the author's investigations. The first twenty-eight pages are occupied with a description of the sexual system in plants, animals, and the human species; and the next fourteen are devoted to a description of puberty and its attendant phenomena, mental and physical. After this follows observations on the sexual instinct and its perversions. The remarks on the latter are as curious as they are unsuitable for translation. We quote them, therefore in the original Latin.

[The reviewer then quotes in Latin from pp. 78–81 and reproduces the original footnotes from Kaan.]

The second part is practical. The causes that lead to *Psychopathia sexualis* in its various forms are enumerated. They are just those with which physicians are well acquainted. The truth of the following statement regarding the sources of this vice cannot be too strongly impressed on practitioners and parents.

[Quoting in Latin, p. 87]: "The most effective and common cause: the direct seduction by nurses, hairdressers, maidservants, classmates, and, to the shame of humanity, also teachers and tutors." [Again, the reviewer reproduces the associated footnotes.]

In *Allgemeine Zeitschrift für Psychiatrie und ihre Grenzgebiete* 2 (1845): 352–53.

44. *Psychopathia sexualis,* auctore Henrico Kaan, medico Ruthenico et doctore medicinae Vindobonensi etc. Lipsiae 1844. L. Voss. 8. VIII et 124 pp.

This splendidly printed dissertation, written with diligence and love, gives in its first part a brief overview of the reproductive systems of plants, animals, and humans and of anatomical, physiological, and psychological development in puberty in the youth and the maiden; and comparative remarks about the sexual behavior of animals, humans, and various peoples. It then defines *Psychopathia sexualis* as a disease of the imagination proceeding from and retroactively affecting the reproductive system. Its second part treats of masturbation as the most frequent type of *Psychopathia sexualis, pars pro toto,* and *Psychopathia sexualis par excellence,* with respect to its etiology, diagnosis, prognosis and therapy. This it does in the usual way, with the habitual exaggerations, mentioning that cure which is at once completely and not at all exhaustive. As of this point in the manuscript, the title should be emended, since nothing follows but a disquisition on onanism such as we already have in sufficient numbers, though some are better than others. Since it can draw no more detailed critique, the present small work only distinguishes itself among its fellows—with the exception of certain not uninteresting remarks found in the general first part—by virtue of being, to its detriment, written in Latin.

The author's Latin is, I daresay, so excessively, ineptly schoolboy-like, full of Germanisms and other defects, that it could hardly be left unrebuked, however little room there is here for extensive analysis.

To what end do people continue to belabor themselves and others by writing in dead Latin, which has become too tight and narrow on all sides to cover our broad, lively present age, even when it is masterfully deployed! As for him who must still struggle with vocabulary and syntax, he would do best to simply avoid it altogether. It is furthermore the case that what is written in Latin will find but few readers in our day. Why can we not finally begin to desist from it?

—*Blumröder*

In *Jahrbücher der in- und Ausländischen Gesammten Medicin* 2: 687–99. Literature.

Poychopathia sexualis [sic], auctore *Henrico Kaan,* medico Ruthenico et doctore medicinae vindobonensi etc. Lipsaiae, apud Leopoldum Voss. 1844. VIII u. 124 S.

The readiness with which I accepted the editor's friendly invitation to report on the aforementioned text is matched only by the unwillingness with which I now dispatch the task. Based on its title, I expected a text richly instructive and stimulating, but now, having read it through with great effort, I must unfortunately confess that I remain absolutely unsatisfied. I would not like to cause pain through censure, but praise I cannot; thus, I must ask the reader largely to form his own judgment on the basis of the surveys, translations, and reports on content that will follow.

As an overview, we will first present the index:

[Index p. 35 follows in Latin]

May each discover for himself the logic of this classificatory system, particularly as concerns the second part.

In the *introduction*, the esteemed author offers, alongside exculpations for having written this text at all, the reason he made use of the Latin and preferred to write "*in usum eruditorum*" and "*magis collegis in arte medica, quam vulgo.*" This being the case, the entire first part, which definitively contains nothing more extraordinary than, for instance, a presentation of Linnaean taxonomy and Eichwald's classification of the most primitive classes of organisms in a proprietary set of tables—up to and including the answer to the question "what is *psychopathica sexualis*?"—could have been omitted. Yet since the esteemed author, in his discussion of the radical cure and his touting of cold water, states that he does not wish to expound on the specific indications and usages of the latter because it is a thoroughly medical matter that no one should take into his own hands, lest he do himself harm, he seems to have intended his text for non-doctors as well.

The following translation reveals what the esteemed author understands by the term "*psychopathia sexualis.*" [Translates into German pp. 81–83][2]

"How, indeed, can it be that learned and scholarly persons succumb to a vice whose shamefulness even the savage peoples [*Völker*] recognize, a vice reason forbids and laws condemn and punish harshly? The reason cannot lie in external conditions, since this vice may be found among all nations, in the most varied regions, at every stage of life, in epochs from time immemorial up to our own days, in people of varying lifestyles, so that but few men might possibly be found who are entirely free from this ill. The reason, which thus lies not outside, but within ourselves, is that morbid imagination [*Phantasie*] which all too early produces longing for the satisfaction of the sexual impulse [*Geschlechtstrieb*] and seeks out means and ways thereto. Should the sexual impulse be satisfied but once in some way besides the natural one, our nature [*Natur*] becomes accustomed to it, and the repetition thereof, driven by the exhortations of a lewd imagination, turns it into outright habit. This depraved habit exercises extraordinary power over men, and the strongest will is as powerless as reason to free them from it. It is the imagination, therefore, that paves the road to *all* aberrations of the sexual impulse. On this road, the sexual impulse is satisfied in a manner contrary to the laws of nature; all types of aberration (as enumerated in the previous chapter: *onania, puerorum amor (παιδεραστία), amor lesbicus, violatio cadaverum, concubitus cum animalibus, expletio libidinis cum statuis*) are thus but varying forms of one and the same thing and all overlap with one another. Those who have committed onanism as boys fall very easily into other aberrations of the sexual impulse, even if they desist from onanism at an advanced age. Among primitive nations the two are commonly found to occur together. In all aberrations of the sexual impulse, the morbidly excited imagination, which darkens the spirit [*Geist*], consequently prevails.

"It seems to me neither incongruous nor fallacious to consider all of these affectations a disease of the imagination proceeding from the reproductive system and reverberating through it; that is, to subsume all these affectations under the general name *psychopathia sexualis* in the broadest sense. In its narrower definition, this same disease presents in adults as an exhortation of the imagination elicited voluntarily, precisely with the help of the reproductive system. Indeed, there exist innumerable stimuli that idiosyncratically inflame the imagination, arouse the sexual impulse, and supplant *coitus*. This disease is that affectation that others incorrectly denote 'spiritual onanism.' I have amassed a number of experiences relating to this question and will expound on them at greater length elsewhere.

"Given that onanism occurs frequently and may be observed by anyone with ease, I have deliberately treated it in this work as the most common and widespread type of *psychop. sexual.*; and what has been said of self-pollution applies also to the other deviations of the sexual impulse, in virtue of the relation of each type to the sex that suffers from it.

"It follows that onanism is but a type of *psychop. sexual.*, a part for the whole, to whose cause, diagnosis, effect on the human organism, prognosis and therapy I have adjoined all sequelae."

Thus, in the second part, we have a *disquisition on onanism instead of on psychopathia sexualis!* The *etiology* is given very general treatment; and an appended chapter, "*de occasionibus, quibus hoc malum exercetur,*" contains less than is currently known.

The "*descriptio pathalogica*" (in which, incidentally, *coitus* is referred to as *unio dynamic-electrica polorum diversorum*) lists the effects on the organism—namely, on the sexual organs, brain, and nervous system, and on the organs of assimilation, circulation, and respiration. In the *diagnosis,* he names many dubious indications, and in the *prognosis* only general (rather than specific) determining moments. His discussion of *therapy* is more thorough. As psychological treatment, he calls for distracting and occupying the spirit [*Geist*] and specifically recommends serious music for this purpose; as for the physical, he states the usual rules, dividing them into the dietetic and the therapeutic. He lists certain signs that would proscribe or limit the taking of walks, finds passive movement and riding to be inadvisable, gives certain precautions as regards sleep (enuresis, he claims, is often a sign of *psychop. sexual.*)—but otherwise, offers nothing special. A litany of dubious medical remedies must now fill up the page . . .

Following a more detailed disquisition on the matter, the author summarizes, in eleven points, his views (not so much his experiences, of which he seems to have few) on the effects of various medical remedies: (1) camphor is only beneficial for conditions proceeding from weakness in the reproductive system; (2) opium does more harm than good; (3) the compressorium à la Neumann may only be used if emissions stem from changes in the prostate; (4) quinine is only beneficial for seminal flow due to excessive coitus and in the second and third stages of the psychop. sexual., and more so for adults than for children; (5) cold water ranks very highly, according also to Neumann and Schönlein; (6) for sequelae, cold mineral springs are of greater help than thermal ones, and (7) more for external than internal use, but always in combination with nitric acids (as at Kreuzbrunnen); (8) ferruginous water is especially recommended for incomplete paralyses; (9) for complete ones, iron intake from regional baths is more suitable; (10) showering in cold mineral waters is especially beneficial; (11) in cases of male impotence, air baths may be helpful. The esteemed author then draws a distinction between prophylactic (dietetic and psychological; the latter involves a two-and-a-half-page discussion of supervisory and precautionary measures), radical, and palliative therapies. In a long excursus (pp. 119–34), he recommends cold water as a radical cure, in particular stating that no remedy may be found that could be substituted for cold water in the treatment of this illness.

He does not detail how cold water is to be used (for the reason already mentioned above). He shows himself here to be as great a friend of hydrotherapy as, later, an enemy of homeopathy. Where secondary illnesses are concerned, he states that *tabes dorsalis* is seldom caused by psychop. sexual., particularly in advanced age; here there is an unnecessary excursus on temperament. What he has to say on mental illnesses is very crude and extremely unclear, so that we will only burden the reader with a very small example in the original: p. 148 [quotation in Latin]. Where sex is concerned, there is nothing that would be worth special mention. In the chapter on "pathological anatomy" he says that he has no firsthand experience and makes reference to Lallemand and Rokitansky, among others. To this he appends the story of a very sad medical case involving a youth about whom the author does not know whether he was already committing onanism in secondary school or only later, in the military academy—the former being more likely, since as a boy he already exhibited symptoms of psychop. sexual. The author then blames the unfortunate outcome of the case on homeopathy as *tractatio negativa*.

Were I to describe the impression this text made on me, I would have to say that it put me to mind of a schoolboy's project. It is undeniable that one may not infrequently encounter within it true and good observations and thoughts, of which the tracing of various sexual deviations to a common cause (even if this cause is not satisfactorily described from a physiological standpoint) is especially noteworthy. Overall, the esteemed author seems to have wanted to use this text to bring certain thoughts to light, be these original or borrowed, relevant or inapposite, which thoughts, in my view, would have been better explicated in a series of small journal articles. The style leaves much to be desired. The paper and printing are of splendid quality.

The following text made a much better impression on me: *Onanism or Self-Pollution, less as vice or sin than as real illness, on its causes and consequences, together with instructions for its cure, for educated parents, educators, or sufferers, by Dr. Julius Rosenbaum, medical practitioner and surgeon, &c. Leipzig 1845. IV and 267 pp.*[3]

If one were to conclude, based on the title, that the esteemed author sees onanism *exclusively* as an illness, one would be mistaken, since, as he notes in the preface, "onanism is not so much a sin or a vice that spreads exclusively through seduction; rather, in any person who commits it even for a short time, it becomes a *real illness*, which in a rather large number of cases arises even in the absence of any seduction," and on p. 230, "onanism is neither a mere habit, nor a mere 'sin,' but also an illness." No physician would deny that onanism must often be regarded as an illness, for reasons of heredity as well as because of the pathologies it engenders; but cases where onanism was overcome in a complete and lasting way through powerful resolve demonstrate that it may also remain a mere habit for a lengthy period, even for several years. We gladly concur with the esteemed author's claim that the many moralizing exclamations of earlier times neglected the important investigation of physical causes, and we gratefully acknowledge that, with his masterful presentation of the sexual act and its immediate and longer-term consequences, he has begun to pave the way to a more natural view of onansim. For one thing, the text is meant for nonphysicians and thus contains an accessible anatomical description of the genitals, a presentation of their purpose and activity, and the physical and psychological changes the individual undergoes in the course of sexual development and activity. Throughout, the esteemed author shows himself to be a fine psychologist. Notwithstanding its accessibility to nonphysicians, the tidiness of the text's form would render it satisfying, and the comprehensiveness of its content useful, for any physician to read. The following passage from p. 13: "involuntarily, the testicles began to secrete seminal fluid" must have simply slipped out in the course of the description's easy flow; by contrast, the subdivision of the procreative impulse into the copulative and fertilizing types strikes me as deliberate.

From p. 33 to p. 124, the text deals with "the *causes* of unilateral arousal of the lustful impulse and of self-pollution." If the esteemed author (p. 34) considers it to be self-pollution when "individuals of either sex seek to satisfy themselves by producing lustful sensations, with or without release of semen or fluids, through the use of hands or, in place of these, man-made implements," then we must assert that this definition is both too narrow and too broad: too narrow because the same effect may be produced by merely inflaming the imagination (in the absence of localized friction), and too broad because any mechanically produced erection could be included in it. Stimulation to the point of ejaculation or return to flaccidity should probably be stipulated as a definitional boundary. The author then treats of causes according to the usual etiological method, like the author of the previously mentioned text, except with much greater thoroughness and sagacity; thus does he consider the effects of climate, of season, of *genius epidemicus* and the epidemic constitution (*genius* = the quantitative tendency of the reaction, constitution = its quality), to which latter point he states, on p. 46: "thus, there will be times when self-pollution occurs rarely and has few disadvantageous consequences, and others when it will be much more frequent and destroy the body quickly and easily, through no fault of the individual. History demonstrates this beyond a doubt." The author juxtaposes this *general* explication of varying susceptibility with a *specific* or *individual* (hereditary) one, which may derive from an overly developed cerebellum combined with an insufficiently developed cerebrum, an easily inflamed lower spinal cord, a peculiar orientation of the imagination, or other kinds of diseases, especially various types of scrofula (tuberculosis, rachitis, cretinism—which, however, does not greatly increase susceptibility according to Maffei). It might not be entirely unreasonable to regard the premature initiation of genital activity as a salubrious attempt by Nature to resist all of these, as it would resist an excess of accumulated, unprocessed nutritive substance (?). Thereafter the esteemed author speaks of certain illnesses to which onanism must be ascribed as a symptom: apoplexy, hydrocephalus, insanity, *angina pultacea,* irritation of the mucous membranes of the abdomen, skin diseases, rectal irritations (worms), bladder stones, diseases of the sexual parts. On the whole, he regards those factors "that may arouse a heretofore nonexistent disposition, amplify a disposition that has, in one way or another, already come into being, or directly lead to onanism in the absence of any predisposition" as proceeding from both physical and mental [*geistig*] defects in upbringing. This means—besides seduction and spoiling—in infancy: milk from a lustful wet nurse, direct stimulation of sexual parts by nursery maids, wrapping in swaddling clothes and washing of related parts, physiological and other processes that awaken reflection (well explicated); in childhood: observing sexual caresses and defects in lessons, schools, clothing (slitted trousers), or physical activity; in puberty: reading, diagrams and pictures, balls, theater, protracted lying around in warm beds, food that heats up the body, being unmarried or completely deprived of contact with women (during time at sea, in prison). All of this is treated comprehensively and with many incisive side observations.

From p. 124 to p. 128, the esteemed author treats of "the *signs and consequences* of unilateral and premature excitation of the lustful impulse through self-pollution," with the aim of painting a complete picture of the same. First, he describes the act of masturbating and its most immediate consequences, among which is this terse statement: "the cutaneous glands of the forehead and nose secrete an increased amount of oil, which *covers those parts in a shiny, greasy film*." We cannot speak to the possibility that this description might provide instruction in how to commit or conceal onanism; we do, however, believe that the esteemed author could have been more careful, especially since, as he notes several times, "to try to catch an onanist in the act is a most tortuous undertaking." Furthermore, certain things may be gleaned from those transient signs whose descriptions are given in full. The author addresses the remaining signs or consequences in physiological order, above all as they manifest in the male body. They are: smoothness, lengthening, and flaccidity of the *praeputium* and scrotum, various injuries to the member (used as localized means of stimulation), urethral leakage, inflammation of the bladder, renal pthisis and diabetes, weakness and paralysis of the bladder and rectum, *pollutiones diurnae* and *nocturnae*, testicular diseases, fungal infections and sweating of the scrotum and perineum, poor texture of the pubic hair and beard, measles, weakness and chills, dryness and itching of the skin, thinning of respiratory mucosa, malformation of the pleura, tuberculous pulmonary pthisis, tightness in the chest, chest cramps, diseases of the heart and the large blood vessels, diseases of the digestive organs (halitosis, bad teeth, flatulence, weak stomach), poor nutrition, gout and hemorrhoids.

Furthermore, he addresses diseases proceeding from irritations of the spinal cord: increased irritation of the spinal cord and of the genital nerves, weakening and paralysis of the sexual parts (impotence), odd sensations felt along the spine (of crawling ants, etc.), involuntary twitching and collapse, tremor of the limbs leading to paralysis, Saint Vitus' Dance, epilepsy, catatonia, paralysis of the lower extremities, syphilitic myelopathy, infection and softening of the spinal cord; similar diseases of the brain, whose collective effect is the destruction of the man of culture and intellect, weakness and irritability of the senses, hypochondria, melancholia and all other types of mental illness and, especially, progressive imbecility that begins with memory loss.

For the female sex, the consequences are, on the whole, the same; the author particularly emphasizes irritability of the genitals, clitoral enlargement, white discharge, irregular uterine bleeding, anemia, uterine infection and cancer, chronic infection and degeneration of the ovaries, hysteria and emotional disturbance [*Seelenstörung*]. In all this, the author, contradicting himself in a strange manner, states: "the female onanist becomes emotionally ill, the male onanist mentally ill; the latter succumbs predominantly to melancholia and imbecility, the former to religious frenzy and lunacy." This sentence, like certain others, almost arouses the suspicion that the esteemed author sometimes wrote with excessive levity.

After the thorough and alarming depiction of the remaining signs of onanism, which could be expanded to include still others, one feels strongly compelled to inquire whether all masturbators are equally susceptible to these illnesses. And to this question even those with completely different experiences receive a satisfactory, if short, answer.

"The *curing* of onanism and its consequences" (p. 229 to 267) is one of the most difficult tasks, to which the doctor and the sufferer must contribute along with the educator. The protocol for preventing onanism derives from its etiology, and it is prevention to which we must now turn our attention. The esteemed author bases his statements on a doctrine that is increasingly broadly and powerfully applied in the treatment of illnesses, to the greater good of mankind—that is, the doctrine of individualization. The author also considers it unfeasible to extrapolate any useful general principles from individual cases.

We cannot engage with this section, which would be worth a detailed discussion, to the desirable extent, so we will note here only the most important points along with our own commentary thereon. The esteemed author states: in most cases it is *not* advisable to force the onanist to confess or to speak to him about his malady. Instead, one must strive to discover the malady based on the abovementioned signs and then make provisions whose purpose remains unknown to the sufferer. (How is this to be done?) According to the author, one can only instruct confirmed onanists, and this only through casual conversation. One should not suddenly and in one fell swoop make it impossible for a long-standing onanist to practice his handicraft. The aim should be to induce increasingly long pauses culminating in complete self-conquest, because the sufferer who does not disengage from this activity of his own accord will always return to it (this is quite true!). The next task is constant supervision (again, such that its purpose cannot be discerned) combined with: appropriate activity consisting in mental work and an exertion of the entire body (gymnastics); careful timing of sleep (late to bed, hands outside the covers, early to rise); of the coercive measures, the author recommends only the straitjacket (gloves and hands outside the covers would be better); infibulation and circumcision do not suffice, according to our own experience. The elimination of the imagination's excitability should proceed, besides psychological means, through irritation of the nape of the neck (with cupping glasses, bathing in cold water, showering—not, however, with mustard, etc.); the elimination of the excitability of the sexual parts should proceed through precautionary sartorial, seating, and sleeping arrangements; by ensuring free elimination of stool (important) and the appropriate voiding of urine, and the avoidance of diuretic substances; and in a positive manner through frequent bathing in cold water, showers, and wave pools (which the author, however, finds inadvisable for female onanists). Drugs not for internal, but for external use (*ol. hyosc. coct.* for injection into the urethra), suspensions of astringent substances, ordinary lukewarm baths—in which, however, onanism is very frequently practiced, as we know; treatment of the skin ("since the regulation of dermal and genital activity proceed apace"); bathing in the sea (in general, the esteemed author nowhere conceals his particular interest in dermatopathology); strengthening of the body through "a diet as unprepossessing as possible, almost a meager one" (here we must recall to the esteemed author the principle of individualizing), in which connection he prescribes a "daily regimen" that includes the preparation of gruel and snail broth. Finally, he warns against nostrums and quacks; it is not so much due to onanism as due to "unspeakable quackery" that "thousands have succumbed to lingering illness." . . . Ultimately, we can recommend this book in good conscience to anyone who does not expect from it the touting of specific remedies; at the same time, we must advise that this book not fall into the hands of young, inexperienced people or secretive and hypocritical sinners. The paper and printing are of good quality.

—Ellinger

Notes

Introduction: The First Sexology?

1. Michel Foucault, *Abnormal: Lectures at the Collège de France, 1974–1975*, trans. Graham Burchell (New York: Picador, 2003), 278.

2. Ibid., 280.

3. Ibid., 281.

4. For a slightly different interpretation, see Volkmar Sigusch, "Richard von Krafft-Ebing zwischen Kaan und Freud: Bemerkungen zur 100: Wiederkehr seines Todestages." *Zeitschrift für Sexualforschung* 15 (2002): 211–47.

5. Joseph Bristow, *Sexuality* (New York: Routledge, 1997), 56.

6. Harry Oosterhuis's work provides an important exception. Harry Oosterhuis, *Stepchildren of Nature: Krafft-Ebing, Psychiatry, and the Making of Sexual Identity* (Chicago: University of Chicago Press, 2000).

7. Bristow, 56.

8. On John Todd, see David Greven, *Gender Protest and Same-Sex Desire in Antebellum American Literature: Margaret Fuller, Edgar Allan Poe, Nathaniel Hawthorne, and Herman Melville* (Farnham, England: Ashgate, 2014), 45.

9. Quoted in Robert Beachy, "The German Invention of Homosexuality," *The Journal of Modern History* 82, no. 4 (2010): 826.

10. David M. Halperin, *One Hundred Years of Homosexuality and Other Essays on Greek Love* (New York: Routledge, 1990), esp. 1–9; Yopie Prins, *Victorian Sappho* (Princeton: Princeton University Press, 1999); Yopie Prins, "Greek Maenads, Victorian Spinsters," in *Victorian Sexual Dissidence*, ed. Richard Dellamora (Chicago: University of Chicago Press, 1999), 43–82; Linda Dowling, *Hellenism and Homosexuality in Victorian Oxford* (Ithaca, NY: Cornell University Press, 1994).

11. Halperin, 3.

12. Quoted in Martha Vicinus, *Intimate Friends: Women Who Loved Women, 1778–1928* (Chicago: University of Chicago Press, 2004), 15.

13. *Herculine Barbin: Being the Recently Discovered Memoirs of a Nineteenth-Century Hermaphrodite*, ed. Michel Foucault (New York: Vintage, 1980), 18.

14. Volkmar Sigusch, "Heinrich Kaan: Der Verfasser der ersten 'Psychopathia sexualis': Eine biografische Skizze," *Zeitschrift für Sexualforschung* 16 (2003): 119–20.

15. Anna L. Staudacher, *Jüdische Konvertiten in Wien 1782–1868* (Frankfurt: Peter Lang, 2002), 1:111.

16. Marsha L. Rozenblit, *The Jews of Vienna, 1867–1914: Assimilation and Identity* (Albany: State University of New York Press, 1983), 132.

17. Ibid., 132–36.

18. At several points, he strongly endorses a homeopathic course to cure onanism, recommending "in the strictest sense . . . a homeopathic diet" (104) and "the serious music of the Germans and ecclesiastic chant" (102) that cleanses the imagination homeopathically. However, in the case of Mauritius S, Kaan bemoans the "inappropriate homoeopathic treatment" he received and concludes from the "sad history" and death of this young man that "homeopathy is able to harm, especially during the first stage of *Psychopathia sexualis*" (160–61).

19. V. Sigusch, "Heinrich Kaan—der Verfasser der ersten 'Psychopathia sexualis': Eine biografische Skizze," *Zeitschrift für Sexualforschung* 16 (2003): 116–42. I am grateful to Ian Cornelius for translating this passage for me.

20. Edward Timms, *Karl Kraus, Apocalyptic Satirist: Culture and Catastrophe in Habsburg Vienna* (New Haven: Yale University Press, 1989), 171–75.

21. Edward Shorter, *A History of Psychiatry: From the Era of the Asylum to the Age of Prozac* (New York: Wiley, 1998), 75.

22. Magda Whitrow, "The Early History of the Vienna Psychiatric Clinic," *History of Psychiatry* 1, no. 4 (1990): 419–25.

23. Eric J. Engstrom, *Clinical Psychiatry in Imperial Germany: A History of Psychiatric Practice* (Ithaca, NY: Cornell University Press, 2003), 6.

24. Ibid., 6, 40–41.

25. Erna Lesky, *The Vienna Medical School of the 19th Century* (Baltimore: Johns Hopkins University Press, 1976), 98–99.

26. Quoted ibid., 149.

27. Ibid., 6.

28. Ibid.

29. Tatjana Buklijas, "Cultures of Death and Politics of Corpse Supply: Anatomy in Vienna, 1848–1914," *Bulletin of the History of Medicine* 82, no. 3 (2008): 570–607.

30. Quoted ibid., 586.

31. Ibid., 576.

32. Ibid.

33. Ibid., 579–80.

34. For the lower estimate, see Buklijas. For the higher estimate, see K. Codell Carter and Barbara R. Carter, *Childbed Fever: A Scientific Biography of Ignaz Semmelweiss* (Westport, CT: Greenwood Press, 1994), 17.

35. Lesky, 75–78.

36. Sherwin B. Nuland, *The Doctors' Plague: Germs, Childbed Fever, and the Strange Story of Ignác Semmelweis* (New York: Norton, 2003), 71.

37. Arnold I. Davidson, *The Emergence of Sexuality: Historical Epistemology and the Formation of Concepts* (Cambridge, MA: Harvard University Press, 2004), 2.

38. Ibid., 15.

39. Lesky, 78–81.

40. Eugen Steinach, *Sex and Life: Forty Years of Biological and Medical Experiments* (New York: Viking Press, 1940), 113.

41. Lesky, 96–99.

42. Quoted ibid., 149.

43. Ibid., 149.

44. Thomas W. Laqueur, *Solitary Sex: A Cultural History of Masturbation* (New York: Zone Books, 2003), 21.

45. My reading here is indebted to Susan Stryker's sterling review of Laqueur's book. Susan Stryker, "Book Review: *Solitary Sex: A Cultural History of Masturbation*," *Sexuality Research and Social Policy* 1, no. 1 (2004): 108–9.

46. Eve Kosofsky Sedgwick, "Jane Austen and the Masturbating Girl," *Critical Inquiry* 17 (1991): 826.

47. Ibid., 826.

48. Foucault, 282.

49. Foucault, 280. The American writer Donald Grant Mitchell's wildly popular *Reveries of a Bachelor; or, A Book of the Heart* (1850) offers a similar and roughly contemporaneous vision of imagination ("revelry") that overflows its object into masturbation and other kinds of illicit sexuality. For a brilliant reading along these lines, see Vincent J. Bertolini, "Fireside Chastity: The Erotics of Sentimental Bachelorhood in the 1850s," in *Sentimental Men: Masculinity and the Politics of Affect in American Culture*, ed. Mary Chapman and Glenn Hendler (Berkeley: University of California Press, 1999), 19–42.

50. Much queer and feminist scholarship has found the constitutive abnormality of Freud's work to be enabling. Kaan's theory of the imagination suggests a greater proximity between sexology and psychoanalysis than is often assumed.

51 Albert Schrenck-Notzing, *Therapeutic Suggestion in Psychopathia Sexualis*, trans. Charles Gilbert Chaddock (Philadelphia: F. A. Davis Co, 1898), 15–16.

52. Foucault, 280.

53. Ibid., 282.

54. For an excellent discussion of the relationship between adolescence and modernism, see Jed Esty, *Unseasonable Youth: Modernism, Colonialism, and the Fiction of Development* (New York: Oxford University Press, 2012).

55. Foucault, 279.

56. Ibid., 280.

57. Sander L. Gilman, *Sexuality: An Illustrated History* (New York: John Wiley & Sons, 2000), 85.

58. Claude Quétel, *History of Syphilis,* trans. Judith Braddock and Brian Pike (Baltimore: Johns Hopkins University Press, 1990), 78.

59. Robert Beachy, "The German Invention of Homosexuality," *Journal of Modern History* 82, no. 4 (2010): 810.

60. Sander L. Gilman, *Freud, Race, and Gender* (Princeton: Princeton University Press, 1995); Siobhan Somerville, *Queering the Color Line: Race and the Invention of Homosexuality in American Culture* (Durham: Duke University Press, 2000); and Estelle Freedman, *Maternal Justice: Miriam Van Waters and the Female Reform Tradition* (Chicago: University of Chicago Press, 1996).

61. Michael Pollan, *The Botany of Desire: A Plant's-Eye View of the World* (New York: Random House, 2002).

62. Lesky, 19.

63. Greta L. LaFleur, "Precipitous Sensations: Herman Mann's *The Female Review* (1797), Botanical Sexuality, and the Challenge of Queer Historiography," *Early American Literature* 48, no. 1 (2013): 93–123. On the relationship between botany and sexuality, see also Robert Deam Tobin, *Peripheral Desires: The German Discovery of Sex* (Philadelphia: University of Pennsylvania Press, 2015), 38–39. On the continued importance of agronomists, horticulturalists, and experts in animal husbandry to constructions of American sexuality, see Colin R. Johnson, *Just Queer Folks: Gender and Sexuality in Rural America* (Philadelphia: Temple University Press, 2013), especially 27–50.

64. Homeopathy also underwrites his notion of a self-reproducing body.

65. Foucault, 278.

66. Ibid.

67. Ibid.

68. Ibid.

69. Quoted in Patricia Fara, *Sex, Botany, and Empire: The Story of Carl Linnaeus and Joseph Banks* (New York: Columbia University Press, 2004), 43.

70. George Chauncey, *Gay New York: Gender, Urban Culture, and the Making of the Gay Male World, 1890–1940* (New York: Basic Books, 1994), 15.

71. Although it does not use these terms, Lisa Moore's work might offer ways to think about botanical discourse as sexology's precursor in Lisa L. Moore, *Sister Arts: Lesbian Genres and the Erotic Landscape* (Minneapolis: University of Minnesota Press, 2011). See also Stephen Guy-Bray, "Animal, Vegetable, Sexual: Metaphor in John Donne's 'Sappho to Philaenis' and Andrew Marvell's 'The Garden,'" in *Sex before Sex: Figuring the Act in Early Modern England,* ed. James M. Bromley and Will Stockton, 195–212 (Minneapolis: University of Minnesota Press, 2013).

72. Ralph Werther, *Autobiography of an Androgyne,* ed. Scott Herring (New Brunswick: Rutgers University Press, 2008), 21.

73. As Michael Marder suggests "Humanity has not yet come to terms with its other-than-human-heritage." Michael Marder, *Plant-Thinking: A Philosophy of Vegetal Life* (New York: Columbia University Press, 2013), 175.

74. On the figure of the male lesbian, see Jacquelyn N. Zita, "Male Lesbians and the Postmodernist Body," *Hypatia* 7, no. 4 (1992): 106–27. For more on *Antic Hay*, see David M. Halperin, *How to Do the History of Homosexuality* (Chicago: University of Chicago Press, 2004), 49–50.

75. The largely parodic depiction of a male lesbian named Lisa in Showtime's *The L Word* (2004–2009) suggests popular, if not scholarly, efforts to limit the intersection between male embodiment and lesbianism.

76. Halperin, *How*, 50.

77. Havelock Ellis, *Studies in the Psychology of Sex* (1906; repr., Honolulu: University Press of the Pacific, 2001), 2:188; Iwan Bloch, *Anthropological Studies in the Strange Sexual Practices of All Races in All Ages*, trans. Keene Wallis (New York: Falstaff Press, 1933), 207.

Part 1

1. We have followed Sigusch's suggested translation of *medicus ruthenicus* (Russian physician) here. See Volkmar Sigusch, "Heinrich Kaan: Der Verfasser der ersten 'Psychopathia sexualis': Eine biografische Skizze," *Zeitschrift für Sexualforschung* 16 (2003): 119–20.

2. *Translator's note:* "Learn whom God ordered you to be and where in the human condition you have been placed."

3. From Epistle 2 of Alexander Pope's "An Essay on Man" (1733–1734).

4. *Translator's note:* "What am I, where am I, and where have I come from?" From Voltaire's "Poem on the Lisbon Disaster" (1756).

5. *Translator's note*: Kaan uses the Latin abbreviation *D.D.D.* that can stand for either *dat, dicat, dedicat* (gives, devotes, and dedicates) or *dono, dedit, dedicavit* (gave and dedicated as a gift).

6. In spite of this promise, Kaan never returned to the study of sex.

7. Kaan received his medical degree from the University of Vienna in 1839.

8. In an 1843 letter to the president of the Paris Royal Academy of Medicine, Kaan presents a manuscript copy of his *Psychopathia Sexualis* and asks that "this little work might be admitted to the enlightened judgment of the Royal Academy of Medicine." This letter is held at the Moody Medical Library of the University of Texas Medical Branch in Galveston.

9. This remark is striking given Kaan's background as a gynecologist.

10. For someone trying to avoid plagiarism, Kaan's work makes wide use of or copies heavily from J. J. Virey's *Histoire naturelle du genre humain* (1824–1834).

11. *Translator's note*: Kaan means to say that this text will be a therapeutic (designed to find a cure for *Psychopathia sexualis*) as opposed to an anamnestic

(a collection of case histories) or a diagnostic (concerned with diagnosing illness).

12. Johann Lukas Schönlein (1793–1864) was a German doctor influenced by natural philosophy and the author of several important books on typhus. Carl (or Karl) Georg Neumann (1744–1850) was a prominent German psychiatrist whose work Kaan discusses below.

13. Claude François Lallemand's *Des pertes séminales involontaires* (3 vols., 1835–1845) is an influential study that linked the loss of sperm (through masturbation or involuntary spermatorrhea) to a debilitation in male health. His "therapeutic" solution was circumcision—both for boys (masturbation) and older men (spermatorrhea).

14. As I mentioned in my introduction, this demotion of pathological anatomy is extremely important to Kaan's theorization of sexuality.

15. The analogy Kaan creates here between nutrition and reproduction is an early forerunner of the psychoanalytic distinction between instincts such as hunger and the sex and death drives.

16. *Translator's note*: Kaan may have confused the term he uses here, *vita plastica*, with the more common early scientific concept of *vis plastica*, which means the power of self-formation and perpetuation of the species at the level of the individual organism. This power is related to the Aristotelian idea of *entelechia*. I have translated this as "organic life" throughout, and will mark when Kaan uses this specific term, *vita plastica*, at other places in the text.

17. *Translator's note*: Graafian vesicles are the mature vesicular follicles of the ovary before rupture.

18. *Translator's note*: Kaan anthropomorphizes the two classes of plants, describing those with clearly visible genitals as being in a public marriage (*nuptiae publicae*) and those with hidden genitals as being in a secret marriage (*nuptiae clandestinae*). This marital imagery continues in the following paragraph, where the genital structures are termed "unmarried" (*diffines*) and "married" (*affines*).

19. Kaan refers in his note to the *Genera Plantarum* (1789) of Antoine Laurent de Jussieu (1748–1836).

20. *Translator's note*: In this section Kaan uses modern spellings for all other terms, but consistently uses *phanerogama* for the more correct *phanerogamia*.

21. *Translator's note*: Kaan uses the earlier spelling *andreceum* and *gyneceum* for the modern terms *androeceium* and *gynoecium*.

22. These classes refer to the Linnaean classification that Kaan mentioned earlier.

23. Karl Eduard Von Eichwald (1795–1876) was a distinguished geologist, physician, zoologist, and paleontologist.

24. *Translator's note*: From the opening of Ovid's *Metamorphoses* (1.7–9) on the development of the world out of Chaos.

25. *Translator's note*: Kaan uses the term *analogia*, meaning here a perfect complementarity of paired forms.

26. *Translator's note:* Kaan uses the term *homo, hominis* to distinguish the human system from that of the animal kingdom. I have translated this as "man" or "mankind" in line with Kaan's earlier comment that only the higher orders exhibit developed male genitalia and sexual organs.

27. Paul Kelleher argues that sensibility was transformed in the eighteenth century from a discourse that underwrites a range of social attachments to a discourse that specifically indexes differently sexed (i.e., heterosexual) desire. He contends that this transformation in the history of sensibility is crucial to the emergence of the hetero/homo binary. Paul Kelleher, *Making Love: Sentiment and Sexuality in Eighteenth-Century British Literature* (Lewisburg, PA: Bucknell University Press, 2015).

28. *Translator's note: Mutter* and *Fruchthalter* are German terms for "mother" and "fruit basket" that were used to mean "uterus" in nineteenth-century texts on female anatomy.

29. *Translator's note: os tincae* ("fish-mouth") is a nineteenth-century term for the mouth of the cervix.

30. *Translator's note:* Kaan uses a technical term, *carunculae myrtiformes,* that refers to the relics of the hymen that remain after first intercourse.

31. *Translator's note: Commissura* is an anatomical term for the point or surface where two body parts join or connect.

32. Kaan employs here the humoral system of temperaments that were used to describe the human body from Hippocrates into the nineteenth century among European physicians. The four humors are blood (sanguine), yellow bile (choleric), black bile (melancholic), and phlegm (phlegmatic).

33. *Translator's note:* Much of the ethnographic material in this section on puberty and sexual development is directly taken from Virey with no citation.

34. *Translator's note:* Kaan means here that the uterus becomes an organ of the menses.

35. *Translator's note:* Kaan makes an Aristotelian distinction (*de Anima* 2.3) between the animal and vegetative functions of the human body. For Kaan, the vegetative functions are those that modern science understands to be under the control of the autonomic nervous system (digestion, excretion, respiration, reproduction). He considers them to be passive bodily actions that are part of our continued existence but not under conscious activation. The "animal" functions, such as sensation and locomotion, are those that either require an active force or impinge on our cognitive state.

36. *Translator's note:* Infusorium is a mixture of bacteria and protozoa.

37. Pantogamy is a system of complex shared marriage in which every woman within a community is considered to be married to every man of that same community, and vice versa.

38. *Translator's note:* the German *Hure,* "whore" or "prostitute." In Latin, *lupa* means "she-wolf," but it can also mean "prostitute."

39. *Translator's note:* Kaan's comments here about the hatred that young men feel for the women with whom they engage in their first sexual encounters appears to come generally from Ps.-Aristotle's *Problemata* 4.10. Book 4 of the *Problemata* deals with questions related to sexual intercourse and its effect on human physiology. The section that Kaan seems to be referencing (4.10) says: Διὰ τί οἱ νέοι ὅταν πρῶτον ἀφροδισιάζειν ἄρχωνται, αἷς ἂν ὁμιλήσωσι, μετὰ τὴν πρᾶξιν μισοῦσιν; ἢ διὰ τὸ μεγάλην γίνεσθαι τὴν μεταβολήν; τῆς γὰρ συμβαινούσης ὕστερον ἀηδίας μεμνημένοι, ὡς αἰτίαν ᾗ ἐπλησίασαν φεύγουσιν. [Why do the young, when they begin to have intercourse, after the act hate the women with whom they have had sex? Is it because the change that happens is so great? For remembering the accompanying disgust that comes after, they avoid the woman with whom they associated as if she were the cause.] There is nothing in Ps.-Aristotle about the women being lustful or more advanced in age.

40. *Translator's note:* Kaan seems to be making a joke of sorts about the development of love couched in the terms of the development of ancient philosophical schools from Socratic to Cynic.

41. Here, Kaan participates in a long tradition that sees women as lustful. See Nancy Cott, "Passionlessness: An Interpretation of Victorian Sexual Ideology, 1790–1850," *Signs* 4, no. 2 (1978): 219–36.

42. Kaan refers to the famous anthropologist Julien-Joseph (J. J.) Virey (1775–1846). As noted earlier, Kaan's text makes extensive use of Virey's *Histoire naturelle du genre humain* (1824–1834).

43. Georges-Louis Leclerc, Comte de Buffon (1707–1788) was a famous French naturalist and mathematician.

44. *Translator's note:* Muhammad is the prophet of Islam; Zoroaster is the prophet of the ancient Persian religion of Zoroastrianism; and Solon (638 BCE–558 BCE) was an Athenian statesman and lawgiver.

45. Matthieu François Geoffroy was a wealthy pharmacist who served as Paris alderman and consul.

46. Genesis 38:8.

47. *Translator's note:* "Tribade" is a term derived from the Greek *tribein*, to rub. Although a marked and rare term in antiquity, David Halperin defines tribadism as "the sexual penetration of women (and men) by other women, by means of either a dildo or a fantastically large clitoris." *Oxford Classical Dictionary*, s.v. "Homosexuality."

48. *Translator's note:* Ovid, *Metamorphoses* 10.85–87.

49. *Translator's note:* Kaan notes here the injunctions against bestiality found at Leviticus 18:23. In a later footnote (n. zz), he incorrectly notes the passage as Leviticus 18:7.

50. *Translator's note:* Herodotus 2.46.4 "Moreover in my lifetime there happened in that district this marvel: a he-goat had intercourse with a woman openly. This occurred so that the men might have evidence of it."

51. *Translator's note:* Trajan and Hadrian were Roman emperors in the late first and early second century CE; Trajan ruled from 98 to 117 CE, and Hadrian from 117 to 138 CE.

52. *Translator's Note:* The poem is originally a fragment of Pindar (= fr. 201) transmitted by the Greek geographer Strabo (17.1.9) in his discussion of the cult at Mendes dedicated to a he-goat (the Egyptian deity Banebjedet): "Egyptian Mendes, along the crag of the sea /—furthest horn of the Nile, where she-goat-mounting / billy-goats have sex with women."

53. *Translator's note:* Given Kaan's footnote (n. bbb) on the obscene collection of material from Pompeii and Herculaneum, he might have in mind the statue of Pan penetrating a she-goat (Inv. 27709, Naples Archaeological Museum).

54. On the association of same-sex desire and morbidity, see John Stokes, *In the Nineties* (Chicago: University of Chicago Press, 1989), and Lillian Faderman, *Surpassing the Love of Men* (New York: Perennial, 2001). For an important article on the polysemousness of morbidity, see Madoka Kishi's " 'The Ecstasy of the Martyr': Lesbianism, Sacrifice, and Morbidness in *The Bostonians*" *Henry James Review* 37.1 (2016): 100–118.

Part 2

1. *Translator's note:* Neo-Latin term for masturbation = *manu stuprare* (to defile with the hand). In classical usage, *stuprum* is any illicit sexual act whether forced or not.

2. Kaan's description of the effects of masturbation in this section are very much in line with the contemporary discourse of spermatorrhoea (which he discusses later in the text). Spermatorrhoea, commonly called the bachelor's disease, was thought to encompass a range of symptoms including nocturnal emissions, premature ejaculation, diurnal emissions, and impotence. The literature on spermatorrhoea is vast, but for a good overview, see Robert Darby, "Pathologizing Male Sexuality: Lallemand, Spermatorrhea, and the Rise of Circumcision," *Journal of the History of Medicine and Allied Sciences* 60, no. 3 (2005): 283–319.

3. Samuel-Auguste André David Tissot (1728–1797) was a famed Swiss physician and the author of an antimasturbation tract called *L'onanisme* (1760) that circulated widely.

4. François Joseph Victor Broussais (1772–1838) was a prominent French physician and the author of *Histoire des phlegmasies ou inflammations chroniques* (1808), to which Kaan here refers.

5. *Translator's note:* There was a prevailing idea that even helminthiasis, infection by intestinal worms or parasites, could be attributed to a hereditary weakness. See R. A. Douglas Lithgow, *Heredity: A Study* (London, 1889), 160–61.

6. *Translator's note:* Kaan later in the book goes to some length to associate this type of specific neurological disorder, usually a symptom of the final stages of syphilis, with the advanced physical stage of *Psychopathia sexualis*.

7. *Translator's note:* Kaan means by *tractatio diaetetica* something close to the Greek meaning of *diaita*, "mode or way of life," a holistic approach to managing elements of lifestyle.

8. *Translator's note:* He seems to mean that a large meal eaten late in the day should be avoided.

9. *Translator's note:* Further in the study, Kaan suggests cold water as a particularly effective cure for *Psychopathia sexualis*.

10. *Translator's note:* This practice of medical binding may also have involved minor surgery and was a "special" practice among Russian doctors. See the note in "Medicine, Past and Present, in Russia," *Lancet* 150, no. 3858 (August 7, 1897): 343–74.

11. *Translator's note: Desmurgia* may also involve minor surgery, but that does not seem to be what is meant here.

12. *Translator's note:* A sitz bath soaks only the hips and buttocks in water or a saline solution.

13. *Translator's note:* A tincture prepared from manna ash (*fraxinus orcus*) that has a mild laxative effect; it is still used to manufacture the laxative Mannitol.

14. *Translator's note:* A drink made from mixing the starchy powder of certain orchid roots with water. It was originally of Turkish provenance, where it was considered (ironically. for Kaan) an aphrodisiac.

15. *Translator's note:* In the eighteenth and nineteenth centuries, sago—a starch obtained from certain palm trees—was popularly prepared as a pudding, similar in appearance and use to tapioca. See the entry in the *Oxford Companion to Food*, ed. A. Davidson (Oxford, 2014), 816.

16. *Translator's note:* a "specifist" is a nineteenth-century term of disapprobation; a specifist applies a remedy because it has been accepted for that disease without regard to the presenting symptoms; see, e.g., E. J. Lee, "Specifics," *Homeopathic Physician: A Monthly Journal of Medical Science* 2 (1882): 456–59.

17. Wilhelm Andreas Haase (1784–1837) was a German physician and professor.

18. Joseph Friedrich Sobernheim (1803–1846) was a German physician and author of a number of medical treatises.

19. *Translator's note:* As a unit of weight in the apothecaries' system, a scruple is equal to twenty grains, one-third dram, or 1/24 of an ounce.

20. *Translator's note:* M. D. S. = *misce, da, signa*. Mix, add, and administer.

21. *Translator's note:* Atrophy of the spinal medulla, usually associated with later stages of untreated syphilis.

22. *Translator's note:* Peruvian or cinchona bark contains a number of active alkaloid compounds, the most famous being quinine.

23. *Translator's note:* Here the lozenge is an *electuarium*, which is a medicinal preparation meant to be dissolved in the mouth.

24. *Translator's note:* Denotes an imbalance in the humors. Here, Kaan probably means syphilis.

25. *Translator's note:* I have translated *coenaesthesis* as "perception," but a fuller rendering might be the internal sensation of a whole organism as opposed to external sensation.

26. Franzensquelle is located in Eger-Franzensbad (now part of the Czech Republic).

27. In the nineteenth century, mineral water from the Kreuzbrunn at Marienbad was valued for its cool temperatures and healing properties. See Leopold Herzig, *The Mineral Waters and Baths of Marienbad* (Prague: Theophile Haase Sons, 1846), 7–47.

28. By "radical," Kaan means an interventionist approach, one that actively combats the disease in an afflicted patient.

29. *Translator's note:* In eighteenth- and nineteenth-century medicine, a *specificum* was a remedy, chemical or other, that answered directly to all symptoms of a disease. In the 1807 edition of the *Edinburgh Medical and Physical Dictionary* "specifics" are defined as "such medicines as are more infallible than any other in any particular disorder."

30. Hydrops is an accumulation of fluid that results in swelling and is often called "edema."

31. *Translator's note:* Exanthematic diseases are marked by skin eruptions such as in measles, scarlet fever, and smallpox.

32. Vincenz Priessnitz (1799–1851) was the founder of the modern practice of hydrotherapy, or the water cure. *Translator's note:* The last part of this sentence could either mean that Kaan had not used the type of hydrotherapy that he observed working or that he has not gone down that path since he does not masturbate.

33. *Translator's note:* The first of only two instances in the text of an abbreviation for *Psychopathia sexualis*.

34. *Translator's note:* Abdominal plethora is a condition in which the viscera are enlarged due to some obstruction of the portal venous system.

35. *Translator's note:* Later Kaan says that it lasted twenty-two months.

36. *Translator's note: Noli me tangere* means "Don't touch me," the words of Christ to Mary Magdalene (John 20:17).

Appendix

1. This review originally appeared in English.

2. This translation from Latin to German to English offers a parallel rendition of Kaan's text.

3. The reviewer here begins to review a different book.

Index

aberration, *see* sexual aberration
anatomy, pathological, 9–11, 154–55
animals, breeding seasons of, 70–71
anti-onanism, 2, 5, 13–14
Aristotle, 185n35, 186n39

Barbin, Herculine, 4
Baudelaire, Charles, 22
Beachy, Robert, 19
bed-wetting, 108, 137
bestiality, 80–81, 186n49–50, 187n53
  biblical injunction against, 80
binding, perineal, 115–16, 121, 169,
  188n10
Bischoff, Dr., 157
Bloch, Iwan, 2, 23
Bocklet, 120
botany, 2, 5, 19–22, 184n18
  proximity of animal and plant life,
  41, 43
Bristow, Joseph, 3
British Medical Journal, 4
Broussais, François Joseph, 94–95,
  187n4
Brückenau, 120
Brunonianism, 12
Buffon, Georges-Louis Leclerc, Comte
  de, 77, 186n43
Buklijas, Tatjana, 10
Burton, Richard, 12, 21

camphor, 111–13, 114, 116, 121, 169
cannibals, 77
Carlsbad, 120
case histories, 2, 18, 86, 87d, 87e, 97,
  155, 185
  example of, 18–19, 155–61
childhood, 18, 65, 85–86, 98, 119, 123,
  145, 173
  separateness during, 62–63
  sexual interest during, 17, 71
chyle, 129, 131
chyme, 104, 129, 131
cinchona, 117–19, 169, 188n22
  inappropriate for children, 117–18
circumcision, 57, 85na, 145, 149, 176,
  184n13
clothing, 83nfff, 85, 86, 87, 104–05, 123,
  151, 173
coitus, *see* intercourse (human)
continence, pre-nuptial, 73–74
copper, medicinal, 120–21, 122
copulation (animal), 69, 75njj
  preparatory signals for, 71
  timing of, 70–71
Corvisart, Jean-Nicolas, 155
courtship, 74–75
cranioscopy, *see* phrenology

Damerow, Heinrich, 13
Davidson, Arnold I., 10–11, 20

diet, in curing masturbation, 99, 104, 110, 169, 177, 180n18
dysentery, 129, 132, 189n26

effeminacy, 21, 23, 117
Eger, 119, 120
Eichwald, Karl Eduard Von, 166, 184n23
    classification of animals, 44–48
Ellis, Havelock, 2, 17, 23
Engstrom, Eric J., 8
Enlightenment, 13
eunuchs, 67nee

fetishes, 83nfff, 88
"first love", 72–73
food, *see* diet
Foucault, Michel, 1, 2, 3, 4, 11, 14, 15, 17, 18, 20
Franzensquelle, 120, 189n26
French tutors, 108
Freud, Sigmund, 7, 8
Friedreich, Johann, 8

Geoffroy, Matthieu François, 78, 186n44
Gall, Franz Joseph, 8
Genesis, 75
Gilman, Sander, L., 18, 19
gonorrhea, 93, 139nrr
Görgen, Dr., 157
gymnastics, in therapy, 106, 176

Halperin, David, 186n
Hartmann, Philipp Carl, 12, 113
Hasse, Willhelm Andreas, 111, 113, 188n17
heredity, 18, 84, 95, 97, 133, 171, 173, 187n5
hermaphroditism, 4, 40, 41, 45, 47–48, 50
Herodotus, 186n50
Hippocrates, 185n32
homosexuality, 2, 3, 14–15, 16, 19, 22, 23, 78, 79, 167, 183n75
    speciated, 18

homeopathy, 6, 104, 112, 156, 160–61, 170, 180n18
horseback riding, 85, 87, 93, 106, 107, 169
Housman, A.E., 4
humors, theory of, *see* temperament
hunting, 106
Huxley, Aldous, 22

imagination, 105
    as cause of sexual aberration, 1–2, 15, 16–18, 82–83, 84, 88, 94, 125, 149, 164, 165, 167–68, 172, 181n49
    opposed to rational morality, 94, 100–101, 102
intercourse (human), 17, 75, 91, 152
    as curing early-stage masturbation, 137noo
    physiology of, 61–62
    recommended frequency of, 77–78, 125, 135–36
iron, medicinal, 119–20, 122, 169
Italy, death culture of, 10

Jews, 6, 81, 84na, 155

Kaan, Heinrich
    education of, 6
    on homeopathy, 6, 170
    innovations of, 14, 18
    in Innsbruck and Meran, 6–7
    in Ischl, 7
    nationality of, 5
    naturalizes human sexuality, 20–21
    religious conversion of, 5–6
    in St Petersburg, 5, 6, 7
    taxonomy of sexuality, 1–2
Kelleher, Paul, 185n27
Kernius, Dr., 131
Krafft-Ebing, Richard, von, 2, 4, 7, 8, 17, 23
Kreuzbrunn [Kreuzbrunnen], 120, 122, 169, 189n27

LaFleur, Greta, L., 20
Laennec, [René-Théophile-
Hyacinthe?], 155
Lallemand, Claude François, 33, 154,
155, 170
prescribes circumcision, 184n13
Laqueur, Thomas, 13
Latin, 2, 3–5, 32, 33, 164, 166
seen as outdated, 165
lesbianism, 2, 78, 79, 167, 183n75
different meanings of, 22–23
Lesky, Erna, 9
libido, 55, 76–77, 86, 153
factors affecting, 76–77, 94
Linnaeus, 5, 10, 21, 22, 38, 39, 166
classification parallels to Eichwald's,
45–48
on function, 20
Lister, Anne, 4

Mahomet, 77, 79
Mandt, Martin, 6
Marienbad, 119, 120, 189n27
marriage, 5, 63, 76, 152, 185n37
social necessity of, 75
masochism, 3
masturbation, 164–65
among animals, 78
as anti-heterosexual, 16
biblical mention of, 78
causes of, 82, 89, 167–68, 171, 172,
173–74
compared to fornication, 91–92
diagnostic symptoms of, 96–98
effects of, 92–95, 101–02, 133, 168,
172–73, 174–75
factors affecting recovery, 98–100
favorite venues for, 88–89
guilty aftermath of, 90–91
gymnastics as therapy for, 106
as illness, 146, 171, 173
leads to other sexual aberrations,
14–15, 16, 17, 82, 165
and modernity, 13

music as therapy for, 102
natural beauty as therapy for, 105
pharmacological treatments of ineffective, 110–22, 127
physiology of, 90
prevention of, 81, 123–25, 176–77
secondary diseases from, 136–49
science as therapy for, 102–03
sleep in treatment of, 107–08
treatment of, 103–35, 166, 169–70,
175–77
wealthy more prone to, 139, 151nyy
see also sexual aberration
Meckel, [Johann Friedrich ?], 155
mental illness, categories of, 148
Meran, 6–7
Mitchell, Donald Grant, 181n49
monogamy, 71
natural for humans, 75–76
music, as therapy, 102

Nature, beauty of, 105
necrophilia, 2, 79
Neumann, Carl Georg, 32, 115–16, 121,
122, 169
prescribes circumcision, 145

onanism, *see* masturbation
opium, 109, 114, 157, 169

pederasty, 2, 78, 79
phrenology, 8–9
Pindar, 187n52
"plastic force", *see vis plastica*
polygamy, 70, 75, 76
poor, 76, 88. 101
Pösthen, 119, 120, 158
Preuss, Dr, 157
Priessnitz, Vincenz, 132, 139, 189n32
procreation, as duty to posterity, 62, 63,
70, 75, 150, 151, 152
Pronz, Dr, 157
puberty, 62–69
characteristics of, 63

puberty *(continued)*
    inducing in females, 64nw
    physical effects on females,
        65–67, 150
    physical effects on males, 64–65,
        66–67
    as predictor of future greatness, 69
    psychological effects of, 67–69, 71, 72
    timing of, 63–64
Pyrmont, 120

queer theory, 15–16

race, 18, 64, 75, 77, 132
Rokitansky, Karl, 10, 155, 170
Rozenblit, Marsha, 6

Sabatier, [Raphael Bienvenu ?], 88
sadism, 3
Schönlein [Schoenlein], Johann Lukas,
        32, 114, 115, 120, 122, 169, 184n12
Schrenck-Notzing, Albert, 16
science as therapy, 102–03
scrofula, 96, 97, 99, 118, 130, 137, 138,
        146, 173
Scudery, Dr., 113
Sedgwick, Eve, 14
self-healing warned against, 134
semen, analysis of, 57
sexology, 2, 3, 14, 19, 20, 181n50, 182n71
    debt to classical learning, 4–5
    descended from anti-onanism, 2, 5,
        14–15
sexual aberration, 78–81
    causes of, 82–83, 84–88, 164, 165, 167–68
    cure for, 166
    diagnosing, 95–98
    displaced onto pet-loving, 152
    essentially a spiritual failing, 146
    as illness, 146, 171, 173
    types of, 78
    See also masturbation
sexuality
    as appetite, 69

    and botany, 19–23
    and ecocriticism, 22
    climatic theories of, 12, 172
    and environmental factors, 11–12
    excess inherent in, 15, 17, 20
    formed from infancy, 17
    hetero/homo binary of, 2–3, 14, 15,
        185n27
    and imagination, 1–2, 15, 16–18,
        82–83, 84, 88, 94, 125, 149, 165,
        167–68, 181n49
    natural expression of, 70
    and race, 18–19
    taxonomy of, 1–2
sexual organs (human), 53–54
    female, 57–61
    male, 54–57
Sigusch, Volkmar, 5
Škoda, Joseph, 155
sleep, 107–08
Sobernheim, Joseph Friedrich, 113,
        188n18
Solon, 77
spas, health *see* Bocklet, Brückenau,
        Carlsbad, Eger, Kreuzbrunn,
        Marienbad, Pösthen, Pyrmont,
        Wiesbaden
spermatorrhea, 102, 118, 122, 184n13,
        187n2
statues, sex with, 2, 23, 78
Steinach, Eugen, 12
Stifft, Joseph Andreas von, 8, 12–13
Suicide, 148
syphilis, 2, 18, 137–38, 187n6
    masturbators more vulnerable to, 137
    water treatment effective against, 138

tabes dorsalis, 115, 125, 126, 135, 144,
        158, 170, 187n6, 188n24
    not inevitable sequel to masturbation,
        135–36
teachers, 38na, 44, 64nz, 72, 86, 89,
        91, 96, 97–98, 105, 108–09, 110,
        123–25, 142

French, 108
as seducers, 87, 164
temperament, 24, 63, 65, 67, 76, 97, 170,
   185n32
   as factor in disease, 84, 98, 139–46,
      147–48, 150
   humoral system of, 140–46, 150
   includes mental and physical, 140, 142
Tissot, Samuel-Auguste, 88, 187n3
Todd, John, *Student's Manual*, 4
tribadism, 22, 79, 186n47
tuberculosis, 95, 101, 155, 159–60,
   173, 174
typhoid fever, 6, 95, 101, 132, 137
typhus, 112, 131, 184n12

Vering, Dr, 157
Vienna, 5, 6, 7, 132, 156naaa, 157
   availability of corpses, 9–10
   emphasis on pathological anatomy, 9
   Italian death culture of, 10
   Medical School, 5, 6, 8–10, 12–13, 20,
      108nn, 131nll

and psychiatry, 5, 7–9, 12–13
Society of Physicians, 12
vis plastica, 24, *see vita plastica*
vita plastica, 24, 38, 53–54, 59, 94, 100,
   137, 142, 149, 153, 184n16, *see vis
   plastica*

water, cold, 107, 109, 110, 114, 120, 121
   imbalance of, 129–30
   important for the normal body,
      128–29, 130
   therapy based on, 128–34, 169–70
   versatility of applications, 132
wealth, 108, 133, 139, 151yy, 152, 153
Werther, Ralph, 4, 22
Whitman, Walt, 21–22
Whitrow, Magda, 7–8
Wiesbaden, 120
Wilde, William, 9
women, 64nw, 65–67, 149–54
Wurmb, Franz, 6

Zoroaster, 77, 186n44